MEDIUM RARE

The Memoir of a Fourth Generation Psychic Medium

by Linda Lauren

ISBN-10: 1492124389
ISBN-13: 9781492124382
Library of Congress Control Number: 2013938458
CreateSpace Independent Publishing Platform,
North Charleston, SC

AUTHOR'S NOTE:

······························

E VERYONE HAS A story, and I have mine. The accounts you are about to read are to the best of my knowledge and memory. That memory was helped along by my decades of personal diaries, journals, family and client stories, photographs, and video and audio recordings. For as much as I have written, there is that much more that I had to leave out. Those stories are either going to be for another book or to share with those of you I will be blessed to meet while on the road touring for this one.

I was taught early on that if I chose to do the work of spirit though the moniker of psychic medium, I was going to have to have a tough skin because there is no standard for measuring these abilities. It really can be a blessing and a curse, which means the person doing it can have a love-hate relationship with it. The abilities are a mixed bag of spiritual tradition handed down through families who are our own, but some of whom we never met. This work I do bears no collegiate degree, and for that reason the profession has taken a few negative hits in the past, and I hope to change all that by explaining what it is that I do and why and how I came to do it.

Every medium will have a different perspective on how they receive information. When I'm doing readings with the other side, I can actually feel like a person is sitting next to me in the room. I can't see that person, but I know I'm not alone. I sense a vibration—like a humming—throughout the room. The sound level of the hum is a good gauge for how much communication will be coming through.

I literally can recognize presence. I "know" when someone is around…like now; I feel a tingling around my head. But there are other ways, too. Like songs, mannerisms, the way my hair might turn out for the day, the outfit I choose, the food I have a hankering for, the sayings I use to respond to someone or something. The list goes on. It's definitely a strange feeling to experience, and it took me a while to get used to it. The point is that by being aware of a lot of little signs, I was able to decode a full message.

I am extremely grateful to my parents for buying me my first journal, because in doing so they started a trend that allows me to recall the events that are more than reflection; they show the body of my work as I grew into it. This was an especially difficult book to write because I miss my mother and father and I miss their stories. I am thankful to be able to refer to them in videos as if they were still alive—those things they shared with no one but me are my deepest connection.

I have strived to give credit where appropriate, and I have changed the names of some people in order to respect their privacy as my clients. As painful as the process was for me to tackle, it is a joyful reminder that I did have parents and I do have a rich past, richer present, and phenomenal future. I get to embrace that with all of you, and I am excited for the prospect to meet you, hear your feedback, answer your questions, teach, and comfort. If I accomplish at least one of those, I have done what I set out to do.

DEDICATION

....

To my parents: Frances & Jerry Gialanella
I love you and miss you. This book is for you.

Special thanks to Major & The Collective for their
love and guidance.

TABLE OF CONTENTS

ACKNOWLEDGMENTS

....

Writing about the aspects of one's life is collaboration, and I want to take this opportunity to thank the people who have been a part of some of that collaboration, especially in regard to my abilities. We meet in this life by no mistake, and I'm happy to reacquaint myself with those of you who bless me with your own special presence.

Special thanks must go to my team:

Susan Dolinko for opening her heart and her home as my sister and friend, and for believing in my work enough to become a part of it as Vice President Extraordinaire. She is often the devil on my shoulder, and Lord knows every Medium needs one! I am forever grateful to be sharing so many magically metaphysical times with you.

Todd Evans for being an angel, and for being there for me in ways that are divine. His special love and friendship has made us family and I am so blessed have him as a business partner.

Jeffrey Moran for being a champion of my work, a great friend, and a very special part of the team. He completes our unique foursome, and I'm happy that he is Embracing the Universe with us.

Gidget Lauren, CosmoDoodle Dolinko & Grace Evans for being the best little psychic companions to be around. Their love means everything and their sweetness made me smile while I worked through some of the memories.

Lou Aronica for his editing insight on the original proposal of this book a decade ago when I had begun the writing process.

Bob Vidal for his friendship and collaboration on my *Graceful Meditations* CD. Surf's up!

Ruth and Morris Dolinko for embracing me into their lives with love, and having faith in my abilities, particularly regarding Linda Lauren's Energy Art™. I thank you with all my heart.

Shan (Psechenichin), were it not for our rides down the "Blue Bic Highway" of the written word, I would never have had journals to refer to in the first place.

Nina Molina-Diaz for bringing the light of laughter into my world. I'm glad we shared those memories and glad for all the vacations we enjoyed. You were a good co-pilot!

Michele Melchionne Kunze and her mom, Peggy Melchionne, for reconnecting in friendship and sharing with me the validation of a reading her mother had with me when I was a teenager.

Jenny, Richard, Natalia (Lia) Thomas Wolski, and Callista (Calli) Thomas for graciously hosting me in their beautiful home in England and remaining good friends for over two decades.

Bob and Beth Monica for their love and continued support and for sharing photos and stories.

Dan Scrocco for convincing me to get my first computer and teaching me so much!

The late William Hickey for his incredible understanding and mentoring.

Carol Cohen and Lou Russo for sharing the energy of their beautiful son, Christian Russo. My gratitude knows no limits where he is concerned.

Little Bear for being such a great neighbor.

Martha Young for her confidence in my insight.

Cosmo Leone for that first *live* radio gig that lasted over a decade.

Bruce Goldberg for his faith and introduction to his radio world with Micky Dolenz.

Micky Dolenz for asking me to be his Resident Psychic and welcoming me so warmly.

Jamie Lynn Drohan for being a remarkable television journalist. I am pleased to call you family and glad to have had a small part in your great success.

Craig Rogers and David Brown for their friendship, and loving energy in my life.

Toniann Antonelli for her love and faith. She "patched" me in and is a wonderful journalist.

Alicia Wakeland for being one of our LLETU Angel Assistants and helping us to create powerful meditation tools at The Center.

Cali Lewis of *Geekbeat TV*, Alex Albrecht, and Kevin Rose for opening the doors to podcasts.

Rebecca, Louis, and Lanai Galarza for being a loving and supportive family to me in both real life and Second Life, through her SL Enquirer.

JoAnn Parks for making Max, the Crystal Skull, available for my clients to visit and share in his healing energy at The Center.

Salli Stevenson, friend and journalist, for sharing Jim Morrison's friendship with me in the past, but sharing so much more with me in the present!

Karin Quayle, Dale Bellisfeld, Dr. Joseph Cervone and Dr. Karyn Goldberg for keeping my body, mind, and spirit happy!

Annie Scranton and team over at Pace Public Relations for taking on such an awesome client and for rolling with it! You're the best, and you get me!

INTRODUCTION—2002

· ·

I WATCHED FROM THE living room window as fresh snow silently fell to the street and crossed my fingers that my father and brother would not be prevented from driving to my house for dinner. It was Christmas, and it was also the first time we were going to try to celebrate a holiday since Mom passed away.

My father had arrived with something he said he found in a drawer in my mother's dresser. It was wrapped in blue tissue paper and then placed inside a plastic bag. I opened it and pulled out a beautiful, apparently old (I didn't know how old), black shawl. I held it up to the light to look at it.

"It was your mother's *nonna*'s shawl," he said in reference to my maternal great-grandmother. "I thought you'd like to have it."

"Thank you so much, Dad!" I wrapped the shawl around my shoulders and closed my arms around it. I felt strange. Warm, yet cold, and I didn't want to wear it, only respect it. I took it off and carefully placed it back in its wrapping. "Too much energy for me!"

We settled in for one of Mom's standard recipes—lasagna—and spent the time listening to my father retell some of our family stories. He began with the present and then worked his way back to stories before he was even born that he had only heard about. By the time dessert was served, Dad had made his way to Italy in the mid-eighteen hundreds and was discussing his mother's childhood.

"My mother was carted back and forth from The Boot"—he meant Italy—"to America because of your great-grandmother's doings," he was saying as I refilled his coffee cup. "Did you know that your great-grandmother was a seer?" he asked.

I stopped the coffee pot in mid-pour above my cup, not sure what he was saying, yet it sounded right. "What do you mean, a seer? Do you know what a seer is, Dad?" I sat down slowly in my chair and placed the coffee pot on the center of the table.

"A psychic, like you, and you get it from her, too. You remind me a lot of what I heard from my mother."

I was confused by this information. I had long known that my immediate paternal grandmother, Anna, had been known for healing and warding off "the eyes," but as much as everyone insisted I came by this through generations, little was talked about it regarding my ancestors and their "psychic" reputations. This was the first time anything like this was revealed to me. I wanted to laugh for joy at the validation, but I also wanted to cry out of the frustration of all those years of not knowing. I had always known that my abilities were inherited; I was never able to put a name on which family members I may have inherited them from. I knew that in Italy, especially back in their day, my ancestors would have been accused of being *strega* (Italian for witch), which was not looked upon kindly. The women of those generations in that world literally suffered for having wisdom that was beyond what others had yet to experience. I am proud of those women. My father tells me they were healers, psychics (seers), mediums, levitators, advisors, babysitters, and anything else that was beneficial to help the human spirit.

All religions are about spirituality and worship, and mine are rooted in Christianity by way of Catholicism. I consider myself to have a Catholic foundation, but my spirit is rooted with Christ in Christianity. I don't judge others, and I don't expect them to judge me. I do not apologize for who I am, how I do what I do, or why I do it. I do not have to justify it either. Just because someone else is not able to do what I know *I can do* does not mean it is impossible. In fact, it means the opposite to me!

I shook my head. "This is amazing, Dad. Tell me more."

Chapter One

IT'S ALL IN THE FAMILY—A FOURTH GENERATION PSYCHIC IS BORN

....

BREACHED AND WEIGHING only three and a half pounds, I was delivered into the world by a doctor in a tuxedo. That's what I was told by my mother and grandmothers for years. They told me I emerged with a veil-like membrane covering my face. According to Italian superstition, a child born with a veil has the gift of second sight and is prone to having psychic visions. This delighted my father's mother, my Grandma Anna, as I have recorded stories from my father about how she and her mother were known in America and abroad as seers, healers, and advisers. He has regaled me with stories of levitating tables and love prayers that he had heard about his grandmothers.

My parents told me Grandma Anna held the unofficial title of "neighborhood counsel" and had visitors who came to her little house on a residential street in the North Ward of Newark, New Jersey. Her specialty was removing curses and curing headaches. Much of this she did in Italian while praying to St. Gerard.

My parents and I lived across the street from her until I was about seven years old. I watched people move through her front door with their problems and concerns, eager for her guidance or a black "prayer pouch" to help ward off the evil eye. I had never seen one of those pouches when my grandmother was alive, but one pouch did manage to come into my possession almost a decade later.

My Grandma Anna had passed away in the 1970s, and I'm sure she left a long list of people she helped. One of them happened to be from my mother's side of the family, her brother John. He had passed away in 1982 in a car accident, and one of the things he left behind was a small, white jewelry box. Inside was a black pouch that had been long ago hand sewn closed and slit open again. The lining inside must have originally been red (the color we Italians like to use for protection), but it had faded to a pale pink.

"What is it?" I remember asking Mom when she gave it to me.

"A prayer pouch. Grandma Anna made it for your uncle to help ward off the evil eye and to bring him positive luck through prayer."

I slowly peeled it open, and we spilled the contents out onto a cloth on Mom's dining room table. The contents were amazing to me! It was validation from the other side that I was born into a special understanding of spiritual communication. Here was tangible proof that my grandmother practiced her own "magic" through her belief in her Christian faith. The stories I had heard as a child came alive for me with every miniature item I picked up from the pile on the table.

"Tiny scissors!" I held the tiny tarnished scissors up. They were set to the open position. I looked to Mom.

"To protect the owner from negativity by cutting it out symbolically," she explained.

"Like with the power of positive thinking?"

"Exactly." She picked up the tiny empty vial. "Holy water was in here."

"How do you know?" Seems she knew a lot more about this pouch than she was saying. And when it came to her brother in California, there was always a fascinating story surrounding him. I sensed one now and felt she was holding out on me. I wanted her to share it! "I'll pour the tea," I said, reaching to the center of the table for the teapot and filling our cups. "Please tell me about the pouch."

"I made the call to your grandmother to get it for him." She fingered the broken stitches on the pouch, put it down again, and looked down at its contents. "Your uncle was having some financial troubles and asked if Grandma would send him something to help turn that around. She mailed him the pouch in the early 1960s. Originally there were the scissors, a crucifix, a piece of blessed palm, a menorah charm, a St. Mary the Blessed Mother medal, the Italian horn and hand, and a small vial of holy water inside. Your grandmother left no stone unturned."

"The holy water is missing. Probably evaporated."

"No. He drank it," she explained. "The instructions were to open the pouch, drink the holy water, and to carry around the other items in the protective pouch for a certain amount of days. I don't know much more than that, except that it's important to note that he had wealth in his life and those particular troubles did go away."

Chapter Two

"PROJECTING" THE FUTURE

....

"LINDA, SNAP OUT of it. What are you staring at?" I can still hear my mother's voice so clearly, as she asked me to explain something I could only see, not interpret.

The time was 1955–1957. Eisenhower was President of the United States, Hula-Hoops were the craze, Jack Kerouac's book, *On the Road*, was on the best sellers list, and my older cousins liked to *Rock Around the Clock* with Bill Haley and the Comets. Meanwhile, I was seeing my first "indoor movie" (so to speak), a colorful array of celluloid magic only for my child's third eye to see.

I remember running into the house with Mom following close behind and into the living room where my father had set up a projector screen for us to view his never-ending filming of his first child (me), and now that my mother was expecting number two, he kept the screen set up.

I pointed to it.

My mother shook her head. "There is nothing but a blank screen, honey."

I nodded. "I know. I have one too. It's in my eyes. Movies in my eyes!" I proudly pointed to the middle of my forehead.

My mother thought about this for a moment, probably trying to figure out a way to ask me in my child's language what I meant. Fortunately, I was around grown-ups for the first four years of my life, so baby talk was not big on the list, and I was treated more maturely.

"Tell Mommy what you see on the screen," she asked as she bent down in front of me and took my hands into hers.

I told her that I didn't see things all the time, but when I did, I would get "the woo-woos," which felt like there were tiny butterflies in my stomach. The only problem was that I couldn't always define what they meant. Today still, I don't know: Are they good? Bad? Are they predictions? Premonitions? Or are they nothing at all?

I explained that the images were on a screen like my father's, but it was behind my eyes and in the middle of my eyebrows. I tried to explain that the "'jector" in my head only showed me things when someone had something happening to them. And then I shrugged and gave her a smile, so proud that I had this all to myself.

So, I'll tell you what I told Mom over the years, as I began to understand more: I see slow-moving scenes that begin as shaded visions of black-and-white and transform into colors as the moving image gains detail. The colors emit from the person's aura like the colors of a rainbow. The rainbow eventually streams out of their mouths like bubbles. To the Child Linda, that was the fun part of having a knowing: the bubbles!

Once the colors in the movie are defined (like on a TV screen), the action ends, and the movie is over. This all happens in about sixty seconds, but I usually come away with brief accounts of something the person in the movie might need to know. Today they call that clairvoyance, but as a toddler, I became pretty distracted by these little vignettes. I tended to be stuck in this "daydream" so long that my mother referred to it as "zoning."

Every time I hear Cher say the words "Snap out of it!" in the movie *Moonstruck*, I think fondly of my mother, remembering her snapping her fingers in front of my face to bring me back to the present.

Eventually, as I grew older, we both realized that snapping me out of it that way was not helpful to me as a medium. I needed to have that zoning out moment in order to receive information.

Chapter Three

GRANDMA & ME AND
A SPECIAL TELEPATHY

....

AROUND THIS SAME time, my mother had taken me across the street for my grandmother to baby-sit me while my mom went to work at her job as a telephone operator. I was mesmerized (and even a little frightened) by Grandma Anna at this age, because I found it fascinating that she did not speak much English, mostly Italian, and that she traveled around her house with a huge turtle following her. I also never knew who to expect, because my teenaged cousins lived on our street and on the neighboring blocks. It was like living in an unintentional family commune. You never had to go far to visit my father's family, and I never knew when one of them would be visiting Grandma, and that was a treat for me. So visiting my grandmother was somewhat of a game.

I walked down the foyer to her parlor and sat down on the sofa, the plastic seat cover sticking to my legs as my dress rode up behind me. I sat like this for about five minutes before Grandma came out of her bedroom.

We did not often communicate verbally, because she could not speak much English, but I always got her message somehow.

However, today something was different. As she sat next to me, talking in her native Italian, tiny purple and blue bubbles came streaming from her mouth. I wanted to ask her to share the bubble blower, but I didn't see one.

As she continued to speak, the colors changed again to white, green, and yellow. I became very aware of Grandma's mood just from the shifting colors. Just like watching the projector screen, I sat distracted and fascinated by these bubbles. I watched them form opaque circles before disappearing into the air. They were coming from Grandma Anna's mouth in slow and steady clusters. I began to feel emotional. The red made me angry, and the green had me wanting to tell Grandma to take better care, while the purple suggested that she was wise beyond my limited three-year-old understanding.

"Hey!" she said, her fingers clipping in the air to get my attention.

I moved my eyes up to hers. "Huh?" I was still seeing the colorful bubbles. "Grandma, can I have the bubble maker, too?"

Her eyes widened, and she smiled.

It was at that unfortunate moment that one of her friends came to visit. All the people who came to her for advice were referred to as friends. I believe that is because that is what they were to her, first and foremost.

"*Come stai*, Mr. Marx?" she greeted, patting my hand and standing to greet him. She turned to me and smiled. "Linda...is good."

Chapter Four

SAY GOODNIGHT, PAPA—
MY FIRST GHOSTLY VISITOR

....

FROM THE AGE of three to about seven, I was having a lot of nosebleeds, with hemorrhaging occurring in alarming consistency. I was also having a lot of lucid dreams with vivid recall.

After a couple of years of this (not to mention the stained clothes and backseats of the family car), the doctors told my parents to consider taking me to a drier climate. So in May 1959, my parents moved my two toddler brothers and myself to California where my mother's brother was living to see if that would help. They sold all of their furniture and made the big move west. We had flown the TWA pioneer flight of one of the very first Boeing 707s, and the airline and crew created a lot of fanfare. We were all given commemorative pins made of wings, along with a little emergency kit. I don't remember now what was in the kit, but I do remember that we took pictures with the crew, and I was chatty while my brothers slept.

We weren't in California very long before we received a call from back home in New Jersey that all was not well in Mom's family. My mother's father, whom we called Papa, had died. Mom held a family meeting with her brother, his wife, and my father, and it was decided that my uncle would fly back for the funeral. Mom would have to stay behind to take care of us. I remember her being desperately depressed at this loss and at not being able to say good-bye at his funeral. This was the first loss in her immediate family, and I remember the day clearly. I wanted just as desperately to make her feel better.

It was early morning. The curtains were open in the living room, and the sun had created a path of light that beamed from the window to the door. Mom sat in a comfortable chair with the Bible on her lap in our house in Sherman Oaks, California, facing that front door. I stood in the foyer watching her, not sure if I should intrude. As always, she could sense when I was nearby, and this time was no different. She held out one of her hands and patted the small hassock to the left of her, indicating for me to sit. We sat together for a long time with Mom patting my hand and reassuring me. A knock at the door made us both look up. I started to jump up to answer it, but my mother put a hand out and gently pressed me down before I could move.

"Shhh…" She put her finger to her lips, and together we watched as the doorknob turned, and the door slowly swung open.

The door was bathed in light, intensified by the sunbeams of early morning. Like smoke, the light began to clear, and in the center of light stood Papa leaning against the doorframe, smiling. He wore dark pants and a white shirt with brown pinstripes, and his sleeves were rolled up, one sporting a black armband. He raised a hand, smiled, and waved. I turned to Mom in question. She did not answer; instead she tightened her hand around mine.

Papa's hand covered the doorknob, and he walked backward as he pulled it closed again. I wasn't sure what to make of this. Had Papa died, or hadn't he? If he was dead, why could we see him? I waited for my mother to speak, which was, for me, agonizingly long, but in reality only about five minutes.

"It's okay, Linda," she said.

"Then how come we can see him? And why couldn't we talk to him?"

"We had a very special visit, Linda. I'm glad that you were here with me, and I don't want you to be afraid."

I promised I wouldn't, but I needed more of an explanation. I remember looking at her and waiting for more. She did not disappoint.

"We received a very special gift today. Papa came here to say good-bye."

Now I could see the other side.

Chapter Five

YOU'VE GOT AN IMAGINARY
FRIEND—SPIRITUAL VISITORS

....

THE MOMENT YOU entered the house, you could smell the rich, red tomato sauce cooking in a deep pot. We called it "gravy," while other people called it sauce, but there was no denying that wonderful smell of the simmering pot on the stove on a Sunday. Even now, I can close my eyes and recreate the experience and be transported back in time to those incredibly delicious and special pasta Sundays we shared as a family. The size of that family varied according to the relatives who chose to stop over. My mother's sister, my Aunt Dolly, was a frequent visitor and one we looked forward to.

"Will you look at that!" Aunt Dolly exclaimed as she sat herself into one of the chairs at the kitchen table.

"What?" my mother asked, automatically putting a fresh cup of coffee in front of Aunt Dolly.

"Linda has made friends already, and you only just moved in." She pointed to where I sat in the foyer between the kitchen and the bedroom.

My mother looked to where she pointed and sat down to her own coffee cup. "It's not plugged in," she said softly.

"What do you mean, 'it's not plugged in'?"

"The telephone is not installed, Sis," she explained, her hand making a waving gesture to the dangling cord on the floor next to my feet.

"If it's not plugged in, then who is she talking to?"

"Her imaginary friend." My mother smiled. "Right, Linda?"

Jeannie Raymond materialized into my life right after Papa died. An only child for over four years, with cousins much older than I at the time, I desperately wanted someone to talk to who could just hang out with me. So, I prayed for a friend who would communicate with.

To my surprise, my mother embraced my "imaginary" friend, and she went as far as to set a place at the table for her. Jeannie Raymond always traveled with us, but my mother asked me to play pretend and only talk with her on my toy telephone. That way Jeannie could be secret.

I'd chat for hours with Jeannie, and though I do not remember now the things she said then, I knew that I was learning something and that my teacher was a guide on the other side.

I don't recall whether any of my little friends in our new neighborhood were making up stories, but one of them insisted that she, too, had an imaginary friend. At the prospect of not feeling so alone in this kind of communication, I was excited to swap experiences. However, while I would give her details about what Jeannie looked like, she couldn't describe her friend consistently at all. This frustrated me and finally one day she told me the truth.

"I don't really have a friend like Jeannie. I made her up. Want me to make her up again?" she had asked. "She's got blonde hair, but every day I can make her hair color and her name change!"

"Jeannie doesn't change. She just gets older. And Jeannie is her real name."

Jeannie had auburn hair that fell into a pageboy style that ended at her shoulders. I first met her when she was my age, but she quickly became an adult. She was petite but very bosomy and stood about five feet four inches. The only things I remember about her now is that she was always smiling and I was very happy when she was around.

I nodded and Aunt Dolly continued to pursue her line of questioning. "You two sure have a lot to say to each other. What is your friend's name?"

I put the phone down against my chest to prevent my "caller" from hearing me. "I'm on the telephone. Can't you wait till I am done?"

My mother let out a tiny laugh and stifled it immediately. "Please tell Aunt Dolly her name, Linda."

"Jeannie." I returned to my caller, and Aunt Dolly swung back around in her chair so that she was squarely facing Mom.

"Jeannie…that's sweet." She lifted her cup to her lips and stopped in midair. "You can tease me all you want, but your daughter is having a real telephone conversation, and that has to be plugged in and fully connected for that to occur."

"Ask her Jeannie's full name," my mother interrupted.

Aunt Dolly shook her head and then turned again to where I sat. "Linda, what is Jeannie's last name?"

"Raymond."

"How do you know that's her last name?"

"She told me, of course."

"Of course." Aunt Dolly laughed. "Precocious little thing, isn't she?"

My mother refilled my aunt's cup. "Ring any bells?"

"Well, of course it does. But surely she is not talking about *that* Jeannie Raymond. She's been gone five years now. It's a coincidence—"

"It's Linda." Mom answered, as though this statement was enough of an explanation. "She's talking to Jeannie."

"*Our* Jeannie Raymond?" My aunt now spoke in a whisper.

I could hear my mother sigh. "Yes."

I had no idea what that meant, but my mother's tone did not sound like it was a good way to be.

"Jeannie is dead, Fran. That's just not possible."

"Ask Linda some questions while she is on the telephone with Jeannie."

Aunt Dolly came over and kneeled in front of me. "Would it be okay if you asked Jeannie some questions for me? I'd love to meet her," she added.

For some reason, that made me feel good. I asked Jeannie and then confidently turned to my aunt.

"Jeannie said, 'Sure, hon. But make it snappy, 'cause she has to get her beauty sleep!'"

"Ooooh!" Aunt Dolly's hand flew to her mouth. "She just said that?"

I nodded.

"Wow. Can you ask her a silly question for me?"

"Like what?" I asked, covering the mouthpiece. I looked up at her, the phone still to my ear.

"Ask her if our friend, Anthony, ever took her out on a date," she said, clearly forgetting I was only seven years old. "Go ahead, ask her!"

I removed my hand from the mouthpiece and asked Jeannie the question.

"Jeannie said to tell you that you already know that answer."

Now I could hear the other side.

* * *

I had not thought about Jeannie in years, at least, not until recently when I couldn't get the theme from *The Perry Mason Show* out of my head, no matter how I tried to analyze it. "Perry" didn't feel right, and "Mason" was no clue. I felt strongly that my sign was hidden somewhere in a title or a name, so I moved on to the actor. Raymond Burr played the part of Perry Mason in the television series. Bingo! "Raymond" felt right but did not give me much to go on. I wasn't sure why "Raymond" clicked, and I had to wait until that would be revealed to me. I didn't have to wait long. A little while later in the day, my friend Sue and I set out to clear up some papers that I had "filed" in a box under my desk. I came across one of my old wallets and started to toss it, when Sue stopped me.

"You didn't even look inside." She unzipped the wallet and looked inside. "There's a picture in here," she said, pulling it out and handing it to me.

It was a black-and-white photograph of me as a toddler, and I was sitting on the lap of my godmother and aunt.

"That's my Aunt Jeannie!" I flipped the photo over, and in my mother's handwriting it read:

1954, Linda and Aunt Jeannie, 2 yrs old.

I turned to Sue and smiled. My childhood guide was back, and she seems to be here to stay.

Chapter Six

WE WILL HAVE NUN OF THAT!

··

WHEN WE MOVED back to New Jersey in early 1960, my mother and father enrolled me in St. John's Parochial School in Orange, New Jersey, where I stayed from grades three to five before my father insisted I go to public school. Located across the street from St. John's Church, the school sported a huge statue of Jesus on the top of the roof, arms outstretched, beckoning you in invitation, while Christopher Columbus stood in front of the building like a centaur.

Each morning started with meeting the class at the church for eight o'clock mass. (We celebrated going to mass so much that I wanted to become a nun!) We wore black-and-white plaid uniforms, white shirts with plaid bowties, short white socks, and black-and-white saddle shoes. I always felt uncomfortable looking like everyone else. I certainly didn't *feel* like everyone else, so why did I have to dress to look like them, too? Rules were rules, and Catholic schools had strict ones that were obeyed or you received a slap with a ruler, among other abusive punishment for what they saw as a violation.

The inside of the school's architecture was archaic. It spoke of another time when scrolling woodwork and heavy gold-guilt frames surrounded paintings indicative of the Renaissance and the old masters. Once you entered the vast entry room, you came upon a long, winding staircase that seemed to go on forever. It was wide enough so that students could go up on one side and down on the other, but there was no dividing line, just kids having to file down in a scramble while holding the railing.

I was terrified of that staircase because three-quarters of the way up hung a beautiful painting of Archangel Michael fighting demons. I had done my best to avoid the side of the wall where the painting hung so I could be as far away as possible. But it taunted me, hanging there precariously in a heavy gold frame, and I could hear it creak as we students all rushed up the stairs en masse for class. It was huge and menacing, and one day it stopped me dead in my tracks.

I stood in the middle of the staircase as the splashes of dark blacks and grays mixed with blood-red skin, and gleaming swords swirled around like a movie. The red overpowered the other colors, and I could have sworn the red was growing larger and thicker, oozing like a film of blood, draping and dripping across it. People were rushing all around me and passed me to get to their destinations before the last bell rang for class and the nuns locked the doors. Once that happened, you were not allowed back in, and they called your parents.

I couldn't move. My feet were cemented to the step, and I was facing the painting, staring, unable to look away. It started to slowly sway, and the creaking sound grew louder. I took a step back as the first bracket on the left of the frame gave way. The second one soon followed, and I remained transfixed as the brackets popped away and the frame began to derail from the wall. The last bracket popped, and the huge frame fell, finally snapping me out of my fright. I dodged it and slammed myself against the other side of the wide staircase to the other railing, crashing into it and several people. Breathing heavily, I dusted myself off, pulled at my skirt, and mumbled an apology to the people I collided with. As I struggled to get up, all I could think of was if anyone had gotten hurt. Finally standing, I steadied myself and looked around me. Some students stood staring, eyes wide, and I figured they were in shock. But something wasn't right, and I could hear their whispers and see them shaking heads. Soon a group had gathered, all staring blankly at me. I heard "Keep away from her," and "Did you know she was left-handed!" (Back in the day, to be left-handed was considered to be evil.)

I drew myself up and turned to go back down the stairs and met eyes with Mother Superior, who was looking up at me angrily. I didn't know how she could blame me when I did nothing. I turned to look at the damage. The painting was intact and hanging as though nothing had happened, and apparently nothing had. Up to this point, my family had assured me that I could help people. How could I do that if people were afraid of me? Were these visions really just in my mind? I saw all the warnings and felt for sure that the painting was going to fall. Why did I see it and no one else?

Mother Superior took me to her office, scolded me for "daydreaming" and causing a traffic jam on the stairs, and then telephoned my parents to come fetch me. Before they could arrive, a very loving sister joined us. She was a favorite of mine and understood me because she secretly told me that she, too, could see things before they happened and could feel how other people were feeling just by being around them. We were spiritual confidantes who felt empathic to the world but were unable to express it openly in public to share with others. She encouraged me to keep a diary of my dreams and visions and was a ray of light in a very dark environment. And she always made me laugh. The best way to describe her would be as a blonde Kathy Najimy from *Sister Act*.

"May I have a few moments with Linda before her parents arrive, Mother?" she implored sweetly. "I feel certain that I can be of some help to the child."

Mother Superior nodded, and Sister took my hand and hustled me down the hallway to the guidance counselor's office. The room was cozy. It had a sofa and two chairs with a coffee table and was full of beautiful plants and flowers. Sister motioned for me to sit down and sat across from me. She adjusted the billowing folds of the skirt of her habit before reaching forward and taking my hands into hers.

"What did you see, Linda? Tell me what happened, please." She poured me a glass of water from the pitcher on the table.

I was still shaking as I brought the glass to my lips and took a tiny sip. "The painting on the stairs fell."

"But it didn't fall. How did you see it? In your mind?"

I nodded. "But it didn't happen, and I don't understand."

"What time was it when you saw this?"

"We were going to last class. One? Two?" I shifted in my seat and looked down at my shoes. "What does it mean? Mother Superior was very angry."

"It means that what you may have seen was the future, and it didn't happen yet."

I brightened. "If we know that, then we can stop it from really happening, and Mother Superior won't be angry with me!"

She smiled and patted me on the head. "It doesn't work that way. One day you will be able to understand that even when you know something, you can't always prevent it from occurring." She seemed very sad at this, her smile fading as if remembering something, and then she smiled again. "You must keep your faith and trust that God is guiding you. Maybe one day you can help others, but right now it isn't smart to share these things, with the exception of your parents and me."

This sounded like a terrible way to live my life, by denying the things I knew. As much as I knew Sister wanted to help, as I think back on it now, I believe she was caught in her own personal identity crisis. She was a bright, thirty-something-year-old woman with the gift of second sight, and because she had devoted her life to the Catholic Church, a religion that scorned her gift of insight, she had to deny any acknowledgment of her abilities. In the 1960s her service to God would be in conflict with her intuitive abilities, but in the reality of what we have learned since, God is the very source of those abilities. I would one day be able to express what Sister was prevented from expressing.

My parents did come to school, but rather than listen to the complaints of Mother Superior, they simply took me out of there and enrolled me in public school.

The next day, at 2:15 p.m., the painting of Archangel Michael fell from the brackets it was hanging on and crashed into the stairs. From what my parents told me, they had heard that no one was hurt. Seems Mother Superior, with prodding from Sister, conveniently arranged for a fire drill at that time, and no one was in the building.

* * *

It was around this time that I began to have lucid dreams of a very vivid nature that bordered on premonitions.

It was 1962. A peaceful row of clouds slowly moved across a pale blue sky, and as each cloud rolled along, it grew larger in size. I watched this magnificent formation of nature enlarge until it filled my entire vision and exploded. The holographic image of an airplane loomed menacingly as the metal monster broke through the clouds, the words *Boeing 707* stamped across its side.

"Linda!" It is at this moment that I heard my maternal grandmother's voice calling me. "Linda!"

My eyes burst open and beads of sweat dotted my forehead as I shot up to a sitting position. My hand glided down to the bed beneath me, and I patted the mattress gratefully, my ten-year-old self relieved to be safe in my bedroom. It was only a dream.

"Are you okay?" My mother was standing beside the bed, gently pushing the damp strands of hair away from my forehead. "Did you have another bad dream?"

"It was only a dream, Mom."

"It's never only a dream, Linda. Tell me about it."

I retold the dream to my mother, and the first thing she did was to call my grandmother (her mother). "Linda had a dream about a Boeing 707, and that could be your flight."

"Does it crash?" my grandmother asked.

"Yes."

"You'd think she'd learn to have these dreams a little more in advance for convenience sake. Now I have to send someone down to the airport to change things." She blew out a long sigh, as if the weight of the world were on her shoulders.

"Well, Mom, at least you'll be alive to see another trip."

"Not till your daughter has insomnia."

My mother laughed. All was safe. It was just a normal day in a very paranormal life.

POSTSCRIPT:

American Airlines Flight 1 was a domestic, scheduled passenger flight from New York International (Idlewild) Airport, New York, to Los Angeles International Airport, California, that crashed shortly after take-off on March 1, 1962. All eighty-seven passengers and eight crew died in the crash. (Wikipedia)

Chapter Seven

MESSAGES ON A MIRROR—IT'S A LONG SHOT, BUT WE'LL TAKE IT!

···

M Y HIGH SCHOOL years of 1968–1970 were spent in the cozy rooms of a four-family house in West Orange. We were living on the first floor, right. Three other tenants made up for the other apartments. The house was pink and white, and, if the neighbors' stories were to be believed, haunted. Mom and I had heard tales of a secret room and ghostly visitors, and that fascinated the teenager in me and the paranormal investigator in her. This house did not disappoint either of us.

It started first with my father. He worked nights back then, and when he couldn't sleep during the day, he would take a ride to the track. He always enjoyed a good horse race and would often go to the Meadowlands or Monmouth to place bets on his favorite horses to win. *The Racing Form* was no stranger to our house!

There was one particular morning, soon after we moved in, that my father found a message scrawled in red lipstick on the bathroom mirror. There was no denying that the message was about a horserace. The name of the horse was one my father was familiar with. The remainder of the message contained the info of where and when the horse was running. The last line of lipstick was thick and bold with the word: WINNER. He assumed it was my mother joking with him. This was his day off, and he jotted down the information before cleaning the mirror, and set out for the racetrack.

Later that day he returned home with flowers for Mom and thanked her profusely for leaving him the message. He had won on the horse! Mom didn't know what he was talking about, but as he told the story, we both felt a need to know more about the house we were living in. Over the next few nights, I began waking up in the middle of the night to a telephone ringing loudly. The only problem was that we didn't *have* a telephone yet! I had been holding out for a new Princess telephone, and my parents wanted to go for the boring, standard black. They were not interested in the added expense of getting a special model just to use as a telephone extension, and therefore they hadn't put their order in yet with the company. I asked them if they had heard the ringing, but they said they hadn't, and they took my question as a reminder that I wanted the Princess phone!

The ringing persisted to the point of distraction, and I tossed and turned until finally springing out of bed to bravely pursue the sound. I followed it to the spare closet that was directly across from the bathroom. I opened the closet door, and the ringing got louder. I peered in around the shelving to the right of the small closet.

A large wooden box was on the wall, covering something. The ringing was coming from inside that box.

The next day was Friday, and while my younger brothers were at sleepovers with their friends that night, Mom suggested we have a "girls" night and that I invite a couple of friends over. My mother was always a great hostess. She would make us little snacks or an onion dip with chips to munch on, and we'd play five hundred gin rummy, which would turn into one thousand as the night wore on! She was the universal mother, always there to lend a hand and an amazing person to socialize with. I loved her company, and so did my friends. To use a vernacular familiar to that time period, she was really "cool" and "hip," and for that reason, popular.

After a few hands of cards, I asked if we could use the Ouija board I had received for my sixteenth birthday.

She looked up at us from across the kitchen table and tossed her last card into the center pile and smiled. "I'm out…And we are not going to use the Ouija board, because it's going back to the store. If we open it, we have to keep it."

"How can I learn if I don't try it once?"

My two friends did not chime in with support, and I understood why. "If you do that, then I have to go home," my friend Laurie said.

"Me, too," said Chris.

I looked to Mom with pleading eyes. It was a long stare, and no words were exchanged. If my friends wanted to bow out, the time was now. But I wanted to understand everything that was happening in the house and to me. I wanted the ringing telephone to stop, and

I needed to know who was doing it. I strongly felt the answer would be in that board.

As a disclaimer here: if your mother tells you not to use a Ouija board, then please *don't*. Even if she *does* know a lot about spirit and the other side, it is not a toy to be used by just anyone. It is not a game. It is a tool for mediumship and should be sold as such. It is a direct way to communicate with spirit, and if you do not know what you are doing or how to protect yourself, you can get hurt. Lower energies can visit you, and they can be detrimental. And even if you *do* protect yourself and use it correctly, there is no way to assure or confirm that the energy coming through is really the person you think it is.

Mom relented, and we chatted with Laurie and Chris and played another hand of cards before they both went home.

"If we are going to do this, we have to say a prayer first. We'll say the Our Father." She walked over to the small foyer and opened the same door I had heard the ringing coming from. She reached up to the top shelf of the closet and took down the Ouija board and returned to the kitchen.

The way the house was situated, the kitchen was off of the small foyer where the bathroom and the afore-mentioned ringing closet was. Mom put two of the kitchen chairs across from each other, and we sat down. From where we were sitting, we could see the short foyer straight past another bedroom, into the living room, and, finally, the front door. She rested the board on our knees and we began with reciting The Lord's Prayer.

"Do you have a pad and paper handy?" she asked.

I reached over the table for the pad we had used to keep score when we were playing cards, and I held it up. She nodded.

"Okay then..." She placed the planchette on the board between us. "Is anyone here?" she asked.

After several long minutes, the planchette started to move slowly...And I panicked. "You're moving it! Are you moving it?" I asked in a nervous whisper.

She shook her head slowly, and we both stared down as our hands glided along the board. "Is anyone here?" Mom repeated.

The planchette quickly moved to YES, and our hands flew off the board.

"I don't think this is a good idea, Linda."

"I want to ask one more question."

We rested our hands again lightly on the planchette. This time, I asked, "Do you have a message?"

We sat in silence for a very long time as the planchette coasted along the Ouija board in circles. I repeated the question, and it went faster, headed straight to GOOD BYE and literally off the board! Just as it did, something caught our attention in the small foyer by the bathroom door. The door was open, and something was slowly floating in midair toward us. At least that is how the time lapse appeared, but it was probably very quick in real time, because the object landed with a thud in the center of the Ouija board. We both looked down, afraid to touch it. Mom took the pen and poked at it.

"A screw?" I asked. "It's a screw!"

She looked up at me, stupefied. "And your point? Because I am still reeling from that thing moving on its own!"

"That's the message. The screw is a very literal message for us to leave or to leave whoever it is, alone."

She thought about this for a moment and then burst out laughing. "Oh my God, that's so obvious." We both laughed, and the whole experience left Mom scratching her head.

"Now do you believe me?" I asked.

Mom thought about that for a moment. "Well, I suppose if we could both see a screw flying at us in the air, then you could most certainly be hearing a ringing phone at night."

Mom called the landlord the next day and told him about the ringing phone and the winning hot racing tip on the bathroom mirror. He wasn't surprised to hear our story and said that in the 1920s a bookie named Carmine supposedly operated his business from the house. When Carmine was arrested, they found his telephone for placing bets was hidden in the closet, covered by a wooden box. Satisfied, Mom reported this back to Dad and me. Much later, curiosity got the better of my father, and he took the box off the wall. What it revealed was an old-fashioned telephone affixed behind the wooden box, wires dangling.

Chapter Eight

LET GYPSY TELL YOUR FORTUNE—
TEEN PSYCHIC

....

Ｗ ITH MY MOTHER'S help and guidance, my
newly developed psychic ability was becoming stronger. Every day was a delightful step
forward into an arena of awareness that few people get
to touch upon in a lifetime. It was at the beginning of
my senior year when I began sharing my psychic stories
with the other students at the high school. Word spread
quickly, and within days I was besieged with requests for
readings. My social life soared along with my popularity,
and even the teachers participated in the requests. One
such person was Mrs. Hanson, my English teacher. It
was during one of her classes that she asked me to read
her palm. My classmates gathered around us, and I took
her hand in mine. A picture flashed in front of my eyes
of two white poodle puppies in a box that was wrapped
with a red bow. I told her she would receive them as a
gift. That was on a Friday. She said she was celebrating
an anniversary on Saturday and would let us know.
When she returned on Monday she passed around a Po-

laroid of two white poodles in a box that was wrapped with a big red ribbon reading, "Happy Anniversary."

From then on I was known by the nickname, "Gypsy." It wasn't long after that the staff set me up in one of the counselor's offices, and I took appointments there. The quarter fee was donated to the school for the battle of the bands.

Recently, I met up with Michele, a friend from those high school days. While out to lunch together, she relayed the following story to me: "It was around 1970 at my house. You sat down at the table and said to my mother, 'Your son is going to have an accident, and I see him between two trees.'"

This last statement brought an audible gasp from my friend, Sue, who was riding in the backseat. Michele continued. "Shortly after that, my brother fell asleep on the Garden State Parkway while he was driving, and he landed right between two trees. He was okay, thank God."

When I heard this story, it occurred to me that there were a lot of readings floating out there from my high school days, and Michele reminded me of that fact by telling me a story of one of those lost readings.

The high school was really close to home. So close that my father used to tease me and say, "Get up as late as you want. All you have to do is roll out of bed to go to school." He was right, and it was a blessing, especially when the school implemented the "Go Home for Lunch" rule and the monumental achievement of "No Dress Code," which meant we could wear jeans! Yes, we paved the way for the present generation to have the freedom of expression that they have today.

The biggest coup for me was being able to go home for lunch. It was an opportunity to visit with the other three families in the house, especially Jimmy, the older boy upstairs. He had a crush on me. I was a teenager, and he was in his twenties already. My family was living on the first floor's right side and he lived upstairs, along with his sister and mother, Carlotta, a short, stocky woman with a full heart and the first neighbor to befriend us. Carlotta described herself as an "outside nun" because she had a huge tabernacle in her living room and she worked "outside" of the church. I had no clue what on earth she was talking about, but I was respectful and always open to learning new things. And her story was easily believable by 1968 standards!

My mother used to say that Carlotta was responsible for the house being haunted. She felt there was something upstairs that was the catalyst, but neither of us had actually been up to Carlotta's apartment. We had no idea what it looked like. All we knew was what we heard from her stories about the house and the ghosts she claimed she encountered.

One school night, long after our house was asleep, Mom and I were still up, playing cards and drinking coffee out of Solo Cups, which were all the rage. I was winning and was about to draw my next card, when we heard a "Thump!" sound coming from the apartment above us.

"I hope no one is hurt. That was loud." Mom put her cards down. "I'm going up to see if Carlotta is okay."

I folded my hand. "You're doing this because you're losing!" I smiled at her knowingly. "You're not fooling anyone."

"You coming?" She rounded the kitchen table and opened the back door that led to the upstairs apartments.

"Right behind you."

"On second thought, you go first." She stepped aside for me.

"I'm your daughter! You are supposed to cover my ass, not the other way around! I'm only sixteen; you go first!"

The back stairs were narrow and dark, with a single light bulb sporting a chain suspended from a ceiling. It looked like it came straight out of an Alfred Hitchcock movie, and it creeped me out.

We got to the top, and she reached for my hand and gave it a squeeze. "Are you knocking?" she asked.

"No! I'm not knocking."

"Then I'm knocking?" she confirmed.

I darted her a look. "You see anyone else here?"

"You never know." She laughed then, her dry sense of humor coming out. She raised her fist for the door and knocked gently.

I rolled my eyes and laughed along with her.

It was Jimmy who answered, and I immediately blushed crimson. From our vantage point, we could see through the slit in the door as he was opening it. The room was fully illuminated. Light filled every dark place. He smiled and invited us in.

"Everything okay?" he said. "You're up late. Isn't this a school night?"

I cringed at the question, feeling very foolish now that we were up there, but very interested in what all the light was about.

My mother and I cast a quick look over to each other, and she grabbed my hand as we walked over the threshold, into the living room of the apartment. Her eyes scanned the room along with mine, and suddenly I could feel her fingers digging into mine. I pulled away.

"That's what we were going to ask you. We heard a loud noise."

Inside the room, Carlotta sat in a comfortable wing-back chair next to a huge piece of furniture. She had the Holy Bible on her lap and immediately closed it to get up to greet us. Candles were everywhere, and placed around the shelves of her "tabernacle" were figurines of saints, angels, and various votives, tea lights, and pillars. Every candle was illuminated, while incense permeated the air, and I recognized sandalwood and myrrh. We told her it was beautiful, but, as my mother was quick to point out, "a beautiful fire hazard."

"Oh, Frances, that won't ever happen," Carlotta said, but my mother had a feeling, and so did I.

"You're encouraging spirits here with all this fire," my mother said. "But, not the spirit of the good kind."

"I'm very scared of the ghosts in this house," Carlotta admitted. "I need my tabernacle to protect me."

"You don't need a tabernacle; you just need a little faith," Mom said.

"I have that, too. The tabernacle is my extra insurance!" Carlotta confirmed.

Suffice it to say, we didn't go up there to visit anymore. She would call us and invite us to come up for tea or coffee. My mother would tell her, "You can come downstairs, Carlotta. You're nuts if you think we are coming upstairs when you are inviting the spirits in!"

Before bed that night, Mom was trying hard to convince me that there really wasn't anything going on up there, but I felt differently. That night was further confirmation when I finally climbed into bed. I had to admit the house was getting to me, and I had two options: get my parents to move or get married and move myself. As I lay in my bed in the small back room, I contemplated what I would do if I ever had that decision to make.

I was so lost in thought that I hadn't immediately noticed a coldness moving around my bed. It was about three o'clock in the morning, and the room was an inky black. I felt the sheet move slowly up my body and over my knees. When it rose up to my pajama top, I found myself staring straight at the sheet, and I could not breathe nor speak!

When I looked up, I saw my mother standing in my doorway. "Okay, that's it! Forget what I said!" she whispered before coming and closing my bedroom door. "Somebody just grabbed my leg in bed! It's time I had a more serious talk with Carlotta."

I was still frozen.

"Linda?"

At that moment, the coldness left, and the sheet dropped down over me. I sat up and looked at her, eyes blinking frantically as I tried to come to terms with what had just happened. "You know that guy that I'm dating that you don't like?"

"Yes."

"Well, I'm thinking about marrying him, Mom."

"I'm sorry. What?"

"I am not going to live in this house anymore. I am too scared!"

"You talk to the dead; how the hell can you be scared?"

"Because they can't hurt me, and we don't know what Carlotta has up there!"

"Well, tell that to the person who was pulling my leg!"

And we argued about the person's identity until I argued myself right to sleep.

As the days in that house continued, I became closer to Carlotta and her family, spending long hours discussing a topic that was close to them, something they called "the spirituality of metaphysics." There was not much to be found in the library or the local bookstore. We didn't have stores with sections like spirituality, metaphysics, or New Age, not even self-help books. In fact, the only material to be found was old, obscure, and considered unreliable. That sounds amazing by today's streamlined Internet and social media standards, but aside from family, there was not much material to help guide me.

Carlotta and Jimmy were the ones to introduce me to *Fate Magazine*, and I wrote for the publication for a while. They often went to flea markets and book fairs. Mom and I joined them on a couple of occasions because we both loved to read. These trips opened up a completely new arena for me in subject matter. Over the years, I became a collector of "psychic" books and bios and own a few dated in the 1800s. (And, no, I never thought I'd be actually writing one!)

So, as unusual as Carlotta was, there was a knowledgeable part of her that had connected spirituality with metaphysics in a way that was teachable. She believed it was an innate part of everyone, and all we had to do was start by a daily practice of meditation, stay well-informed, pray, and be open to helping others. My mother liked her teachings because it used a person's religion as their foundation while helping them to understand the ways of spirit. The only thing she added, which Carlotta apologized for omitting, was to remember to be grateful. That's when I adopted the attitude of gratitude. I imagine it would be safe to say that they all helped me become more well-rounded, because I was exposed to so many subjects that I would have otherwise missed. These are the people who wound up giving me the basis for my psychic awareness.

About five years later, just as Mom had predicted, the second floor of that house was engulfed by smoke due to the amount of candles and the faulty wiring in the walls, forcing everyone out. I was a newlywed at the time, and on the night of the fire, my family camped out on the floor of our apartment in the next town. They soon moved, relocating to a one-family house.

Chapter Nine

MY FIRST SÉANCE

·······································

S O HOW DOES a fourth generation psychic medium
disobey her mother? She has a séance before she
is old enough to facilitate one! That was what I did
back in 1969, because I was a new kid in a new school
who was "different," and I wanted to make friends.
Someone suggested that we have a séance at our friend
Seth's house and that we try to speak with the great ma-
gician and escape artist Harry Houdini. They asked me
to show them the way.

Seth lived in a stately house in the old and once pres-
tigious Seven Oaks section of the Oranges in New Jersey.
The homes there were large mansions that were no longer kept in the grand style that surrounded them in the
1800s, but they were still in decent (in some cases, stel-
lar) condition. My then boyfriend picked me up on his
bicycle (yes, a bicycle), and we rode over to Seven Oaks.
I was pretty excited because, just shy of seventeen, I was
finally going to facilitate my first séance, something my
mother considered out of the question.

I remember standing there beside my boyfriend while he rang the doorbell. We could hear Seth bounding down the stairs, and waited as he pulled open the heavy oak door. "Come on in! I'm all set up."

As we stepped into the large entry, my eyes immediately swept up to a beautiful tapestry of angels that hung over the staircase in welcome. The long staircase led to the other floors of the house, with the dining room on the immediate right, and across the hall the living room was to the left.

"Everyone is here. I have us sitting at the dining room table," Seth said.

I remember hearing him, but I became lost in the swirls of the color in the tapestry, and soon his voice was barely audible to me. Before I realized it, I was walking up the staircase with slow, deliberate steps. The closer I came to the next landing, the more distant the voices became. I stopped at the second landing and reached out to hold the railing as dizziness gripped me. My eyes started tearing, and my throat closed up, and I felt like I could not breathe. I steadied myself and continued up to the next landing. It was here that my peripheral vision disappeared, and I found myself walking into a tunnel of the white light that surrounded me. I stopped as an image began to take form. The white turned to dark and then light again. That's when I saw her more clearly. Standing outside the door where I had stopped was a woman dressed all in black. And she didn't look very pleased to see me!

Her salt-and-pepper hair was pulled away from her face and tied into a long braid. I opened my mouth to speak, but nothing came out. She was not smiling, and her hands were folded in front of her. I froze. We made eye contact, and I found myself running back down those steps faster than I knew was possible. I stumbled right down into the surprised arms of my boyfriend at the bottom.

"You didn't tell me your grandmother was home, Seth," I reprimanded, trembling. "She was pretty angry that I went upstairs. She scared me. I didn't expect her—"

"Huh?" Seth looked at us. "Didn't you tell her?" He raised an eyebrow in question to my boyfriend.

"Tell me what?" I was sitting on the bench in the foyer and was finally feeling my heavy breathing subside.

"That's why you're here. My grandmother died yesterday—there is no way that you saw her alive just now up on the third floor. We thought you might want to call her to talk to us when you call Houdini."

That is all I remember hearing before I slumped back against the bench and fainted.

Séance called on account of fright!

47

Grandma's Pouch

Little Linda with Grandma Anna

**Little Linda on the phone
with Jeannie**

Little Linda with Mom

Linda with Dad

Grandparents Maria and Ralph

**Linda in her
St. John Uniform**

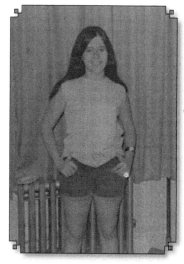

**Teen Psychic with her
Crystal Ball Ring**

Chapter Ten

NEAR-DEATH EXPERIENCE—THE OTHER SIDE AND BACK

···

FROM PUBERTY, I had suffered from a condition called endometriosis, and for a long time it was held at bay through medication. As I neared my thirtieth birthday, the condition began to flare up again, and I was rushed to the hospital because of intense pain. My parents came along to lend their support, and I was rushed into surgery soon after arriving. I'm told several hours went by before I came to. When I did, it was to the prayers of a priest who was standing over my hospital bed giving me the last rites. The rest of the details from my parents were sketchy as they were trying to keep most of this from me for what they said was for my own protection. My mother said "several minutes" had gone by in the operating room during which I was gone.

But I didn't spend those minutes on the operating table.

I remember the light was bright, and I recognized the long tunnel the moment it came into view. When I looked down this tunnel, I could see shapes of people, and soon I recognized them as well. I remember seeing my Grandma Anna, my Aunt Fran, and my Great-Uncle Joe. I remembered, too, that they were also all dead. But that bright light beckoned me forward, filling me with a warm, comforting, and peaceful feeling unlike anything I had ever felt before. I wanted to go to that light. I wanted that peace. But as those "several minutes" came to an end, I sensed myself being pulled back to the table, and the tunnel disappeared. The next I recalled, I was opening my eyes to my mother squeezing my hand and crying in obvious relief.

It is difficult to put into words what this experience meant to me, except to say that it made me appreciate the precious moments we have available to us and that there is a place awaiting us that is comforting and filled with the love of those who passed before us. It was such a traumatic experience for me that I shut psychic matters from my life for more than a decade while I came to terms with it.

This near-death experience was a catalyst for whatever intuitive vibes I had been suppressing during my marriage. My then husband was not a fan of what I could do and didn't want me to even mention it. My way around that was to continue to keep journals on what I was feeling and experiencing so that I could chart my progress secretly.

Chapter Eleven

ACTING OUT—THE HONOR
OF HIS MENTORSHIP

·······································

I SAT MESMERIZED BY the long ash of his Parliament cigarette as it dangerously grew in length. I waited for it to fall, but it didn't. Instead, he flicked it into the ashtray in front of him and used it to light a new cigarette from the pack. We were seated in the crowded basement of HB Actors Studio in Greenwich Village, New York. William Hickey (a veteran character actor most noted for later winning the Oscar for *Prizzi's Honor* and acting in films like *Little Big Man* and *National Lampoon's Christmas Vacation*) was telling us to not be afraid to "dig deep inside" for what we needed for an emotional scene.

As acting schools go, New York has always had a rich source to choose from. When I set out to research acting schools, I was considering those that were less like a university and more like life. Those power three were: Herbert Berghof/Uta Hagen of HB Studios, Stella Adler, and the Elia Kazan/Lee Strasberg's Actors Studio teaching The Stanislavsky Method. I didn't care for The Method, and I didn't feel a connection to Stella Adler either. HB offered the most diversity in time, teachers, and the curriculums. I wasn't saddled by "school hours," which meant that class could be at 8:00 a.m. or 2:00 a.m. because there was always someone teaching. It was the perfect fit for a working professional and newlywed to schedule. And I loved walking through the village after class with some of the others, stopping at cafés for a glass of wine or a light dinner. There was a restaurant on Bleecker Street that some of the actors went to often. We would secure a table under the awning if it was a nice day (or a corner table inside), and I would read their palms for fun, or share what I "saw" as we hung out. It was mostly in fun, as I had resigned myself to the fact that the way to deal with my intuitive talents was to hide it from my husband and share it with a handful of people. That's as "public" as I went with it.

I had been working with William Hickey as my acting coach for a while, attending his classes each Saturday afternoon. It was not so much that I had an aspiration to make my way in the world as an actress, as much as I felt I could learn how to deal with emotion and how best to convey it. I wanted to work with my sense of "feeling," and this was a step I took toward that. If a part came my way, I would definitely be happy about it, but that was not my primary goal, much to Mr. Hickey's frustration.

I had stayed away from HB Studios for a while, while I sorted out how I felt about who I was and the direction I was going. I was in panic mode from having been mugged earlier that month. It was an uncomfortable way to live, and I forced myself to take the bus ride into Manhattan from our Jersey home to make a first step toward self-healing by resurfacing to connect with people beside immediate family. This was my first day back. Bill Hickey knew that I was married and that I was desperately trying to downplay or "hide" my psychic abilities. He felt it was vital that I use it as much as possible. I was at a paranormal crossroads as a result of my marriage, and he completely understood my dilemma, but being older, and thus wiser, he begged to differ. To that end, he made sure I was involved in most of the acting exercises we did in class.

"Welcome back. You are just in time to join us for a field trip today."

The ash fell, and my reverie was broken as I became alert, grateful that we would be out of the hot basement. It was warm, and there had been no air. My hair was long, way beyond my waist, and I hadn't tied it up, which only made me feel hotter.

A minibus was idling curbside, and the eight of us in attendance piled inside, our esteemed teacher picking up the rear. He sat down and swiveled his body to face us on the bus.

"We're going to the theater!" he announced, a new Parliament hanging at the edge of his lip.

The "theater" turned out to be a few blocks over from where we were, and we piled back out and up the stairs of a brownstone to the rooftop. We were ushered into a room with chairs lined up and scrambled for a seat. It was here that our esteemed teacher taught us how to fall through a door when someone opens it on the other side. One person would be the door opener, the other the victim. It was supposed to teach us two things: the correct way to fall flat on your face without getting hurt, and trust, which is what one needed to do the fall in the first place. It was not an exercise I was looking forward to.

"Watch carefully," he said, the cigarette tip rocking up and down as it magically stuck to his bottom lip. "I'm going to go through this door and fall forward, as though I'm dead."

I eagerly watched him, eyebrows raised, hoping he had enough sense to take the butt from his lips, which he did before opening the door and stepping into the hallway. From my vantage point to the right of the door, it was a few moments later that we heard him gently knock. No one got up. He neglected to tell us who was participating with him in the exercise, which left us looking around the room to each other for guidance. He knocked again, this time more persistently. The room was hot and without air, and the building was old. The longer this exercise took, the more oppressive the heat was going to get. When no one answered him, I got up to do it.

My hand on the knob, I opened the door, and Bill Hickey fell forward, and I had the automatic reaction of jumping back and away from him so he didn't fall on me. He got to his feet, none the worse for wear.

"Let's try just opening the door with no one on the other side and see if you can repeat the movement as an actor." His tiny, clipped, and smoke-ravaged voice cackled at the delight that we would be attempting this. "Linda, since you're standing there already, let's see if you can repeat your movement." He lit a Parliament.

"Go head. Open the door. And remember, even though there is no one on the other side, you do not know that, because you will still be hearing a knock."

I nodded and then positioned myself in front of the door as the other students looked on. When Bill gave a knock sound, I slowly opened the door to the darkness and, after a few moments, jumped back. He shook his head and asked me to do it again. The second time bore the same results, but it was the third that caused me anxiety.

"One more time. And I want you to communicate to your head who might be on the other side of that door. *See* that person!"

I groaned and then wanly smiled as I positioned myself squarely in front of the door. I closed my eyes, cleared my head, and took a deep breath. I could feel energy building up in the hallway, a decidedly masculine energy. We were in an old brownstone in New York that had its own ghostly history. I wasn't sure what to make of it, but I felt I was about to briefly meet someone long deceased from another time.

"Linda, please open the door!" Bill repeated.

I opened my eyes and swung the door open. The hallway was dark, but the figure was clear, and in front of me was a man in a black hat and a black cloak, and he was carrying a cane. I could hear Bill Hickey talking to me like faint background sound to complete the exercise, but I stood frozen, my hand glued to the doorknob. The man smiled, tipped his cane to his hat, a top hat, and then reached forward as if to give me the cane. I had completely blocked out the classroom, and it was just this stranger and me.

The movement of the cane toward me made me jump back quickly to shut the door. I slammed it hard, and I was breathing heavily. Our teacher was highly intuitive himself, and class was dismissed for us to think this last demonstration over. He didn't dismiss me right away, however. Instead, he asked me to join him at a local café for something cold. He had invited two of his assistants along with us.

"What did you see?" he asked after ordering, leaning forward to light another cigarette.

"I saw a man in a black cloak, top hat, and cane. I froze when I saw him."

"Yes, we saw that."

"You saw him, too?"

"No...We saw you freeze."

"Well, he reached out to me with his cane, and I didn't want it to touch me, so I stepped back quickly and closed the door."

They all nodded and Bill said, "Don't lose that. It's a gift."

I knew what he meant. I knew the man in black was a ghost. I just didn't know what he wanted or how/if I should help him.

Chapter Twelve

MY CALIFORNIA DREAMING

······································

IT WAS THE summer of 1977, and I was newly divorced. I took off for California at the invitation of that same uncle who helped me when I was getting all those nosebleeds as a child. I worked on some television scripts and enjoyed a very posh lifestyle in Malibu, living in one of Liberace's beach houses. But, nothing prepared me for the honor of hearing Mr. Liberace play his baby white grand piano in the living room before the piano was moved. He was possessed of a very generous spirit. I sat on the red velvet sofa beside my uncle and grand-mother as he played a little tune. I later wrote it into my journal with excitement. I had never heard "Clair de Lune" and "Chopsticks" played together and sound so incredible! It was short and sweet. My face was wet with tears of joy that day and I will hold that magical moment in time close to my heart.

I was in culture shock, and my focus since the near-death experience had been on living, and I set out to create a career as a writer/actress. That doesn't mean that the psychic aspects of my life disappeared.

They came about in a very matter-of-fact manner, and for that reason, I didn't realize I was even "reading" people. This was the best that could have been offered to me at the time in the continued training ground.

"Let's take a walk along the beach!"

My uncle was coming down the stairs with quick steps, his mood up, and he was eager to attack the day. He was the "rich uncle in California" who everyone talked about and focused on. I knew him from visits, but not very well. To be with him was like having an audience with someone of intense power, and there was no mistaking that. He was someone I had looked up to and hoped to learn from.

I looked at him now. His dark hair was combed and his face clean-shaven, but he was still in his robe. I watched as he rounded the corner into the kitchen and headed for the coffee brewer. He was handsome, and at a fit, health-food conscious fifty-two, he looked nice even when in lounging attire.

"Well?" He smiled through sparkling white teeth that made me want to meet his dentist as soon as possible. "I can introduce you to some of the neighbors. They're good friends."

I was sitting at the counter in the Malibu beach house, wearing a pair of micro-short cutoffs and a Malibu T-shirt.

"Sounds good! But aren't you going to get dressed?"

"I *am* dressed." He poured himself a cup and took a sip of the dark coffee, and I followed him to the crystal-beaded curtains that covered the glass doors that made up almost the entire back of the house. Or was it the front of the house? I was never quite sure because the gates were on the Pacific Coast Highway side as well as the beach side. Though, it was confirmed to me that the front was the PCH side when I inadvertently locked myself out and didn't have the alarm code. Within seconds I was facing the barrels of not one, but three shotguns, because they thought I had breached the security alarm. (My hat off to them, but that was one very scary experience.)

My uncle paused before sliding the doors open and reached down into the drawer of one of the end tables. "I never walk the beach alone." He tucked a tiny ivory- and pearl-handled gun into his robe pocket, and we headed down the stairs to the ocean.

The sun was bright, and it already felt hot, but not humid. The next house was relatively close and owned by someone my uncle introduced me to as Little Bear. I had already met Little Bear on a previous occasion when she was locked out of her house by her roommate and chose our glass doors to bang on for refuge. At first I thought I was seeing a ghost, because she was all in white, including her hair. But my uncle assured me she very real, very rich, very eccentric, a very good friend, and that I could trust her.

I followed him up the back path to Little Bear's not-so-little house, and we were greeted warmly considering that it was only five forty-five in the morning! Uncle was an early riser (or a late sleeper, depending on how you looked at it), and party people like Little Bear were just arriving home at that time, so it was the best time to visit.

This would be the first of many beach walks and many visits with some very powerful people. I realized quickly that my uncle was utilizing my ability and how these were my first real clients.

Further up the beach was a Beverly Hills jewelry designer who had known my uncle for a decade. I remember sitting at her kitchen counter while her house was being renovated and under heavy construction, and giving her my take on the architectural plans! And so it went with each house, each business, each real estate venture, and each visit. If experience was the best teacher, mine deserved a golden apple for showing me the way to work with what I felt people should know based on the questions they posed to me.

At the suggestion of Bill Hickey back East, I had a brief stay with the Tracy Roberts Acting School in Beverly Hills, but I realized that though I enjoyed writing, memorizing scripts for acting was simply not working for me. Helping to write television scripts was a great start because I had a passion for the written word. I enjoyed meeting stars and celebrities, but the lifestyle was too fast paced, my uncle was too possessive, and the industry of the West Coast did not hold the same enthusiasm I thought it would at the time.

I always told my parents that I felt I was meant for "something more" but that I didn't know yet what that "something more" was. What I did know was that relocating to California was not the answer. I took a plane back home to New Jersey to strategize.

Chapter Thirteen

MARTHA'S VINEYARD, 1989

· ·

O NCE A YEAR I planned a weeklong trip with my friend, Nina, around Labor Day weekend for some rest, relaxation, and maybe a paranormal experience. She was a perfect traveling companion for this because she was a good navigator and always ready for the next psychic adventure.

Our only requirement was to be by water, because it was a priority and necessary to feed my personal soul's desire. The choice always included a clean white beach and cool ocean waves washing the shore, and since I was the one who owned a car, I was the designated driver.

I picked up my friend and, with the help of her husband, loaded up my hatchback and headed for our first trip to quiet Martha's Vineyard. We had made arrangements to stay at a quaint bed-and-breakfast around the area of Oak Bluffs and looked forward to the drive. At the time we were both working together for a legal firm, and my job in particular was pretty heavy-duty, so we were tired and eager for this relaxation with a nice ocean view. We quickly found out that in Oak Bluffs that if you didn't want to be thought of as a tourist you would refer to the city as OB. At least that's what the natives told us at the nearest restaurant. We had stopped in because it was called Linda Jeans, and I often look for restaurants that have my name in places that might be haunted. I found both in OB.

We caught the last ferry over from Woods Hole and made our way to the inn, a beautiful Cape Cod, every room a different shade of pink. We were staying in the captain's suite, which was assessable via the wraparound porch. We were not aware of that and arrived at eleven o'clock in the evening, right through the front door of the inn. We were tired and drained from the long ride and just wanted to settle in. It didn't dawn on either of us to look for a note of any kind. So when no one came down to greet us at this very late hour, I reached for the string of the huge cow bell that was in the entryway and yanked on the rope a couple of times. My friend held her hands up to her ears to cover them.

"It's loud!"

Before I could answer, a woman rushing down the stairs in a slow-moving panic broke our conversation. "Please don't ring it again. We don't want to wake the other guests. Didn't you see my note?"

We turned and were faced with a woman of about five foot five, with very thick, long, wavy white hair. She had obviously been sleeping because she was in a nightgown, and she was doing her best to wrap her robe quickly around her.

"We are so sorry! We didn't see the note!"

We introduced ourselves, and the woman walked over to the counter and sighed. Hanging from a string and easily visible was a note written on the outside of an envelope telling us to go around the side of the house to our suite. She would see us in the morning, and the key was inside the envelope. Embarrassed, we said good night, apologized again, and went to get our bags so that we could retire for the evening.

As tired as I was, the excitement of the trip would not allow me to unwind. So I stayed there in the dark, eyes closed, doing some meditative breathing, hoping to fall asleep before daylight. I inhaled and exhaled slowly and listened to the sound of my breathing, hoping it would quickly deepen into slumber. That's when I heard it, a soft whisper in my ear. The light beside the bed moved at least three inches away from me on the end table and turned itself on! My first thought was to attribute the light going on to a faulty socket or loose wire. I never ever think something is paranormal first. I'm always the skeptic until proven otherwise. And hearing voices was really not something new to me, as I had heard them before. It's inherent to who I am.

I shut off the light, closed my eyes again, and turned over on my side. I restarted my deep breathing, and once again I heard the whisper. It was definitely a woman's voice, but I couldn't understand what she was saying. Again, the lamp moved, and the light came on! Only this time it was accompanied by an almost inaudible scream from my friend on the other side of the room.

"Did you just see that lamp move?" Her hand flew to her mouth.

"Yes. And I've also been hearing voices."

"I'm glad were only staying here three days before we move up the Cape."

Moving up the Cape meant we were headed out to Provincetown. In 1989, Provincetown was a mecca known for the many writers and artistic people who had converged to create a community and colonies of like-minded individuals. The quaint and lovely tip of Cape Cod was the frequent haunt of people like Norman Mailer, who wrote all his books there. Having just finished reading one of them, I was curious to walk across the same paths where his vibration was at its creative height.

It was in Provincetown that we met the vacationing Thomas family. Richard and Jenny Thomas had come from England along with their two children, Lia, a teenager, and Calli, who was a toddler of three. They had the room next door to mine, which was next door to my friend Nina's. A wrap-a-round deck connected it all, and little Calli had wandered into my open door. An inquisitive child, she began a series of questions about the things we were unpacking. She had a sweet English accent and every question began with, "And what is that?" She was not satisfied until she got her answer, so you had to tell her what it was she was pointing at. She delighted us as she boldly walked into the room and sat on the bed, immediately attracted to my friend's people pillow that we named Herbie. It was only a few seconds before that her mother, Jenny, came in with Lia to fetch the baby. We became immediate friends and fell into spending the rest of that vacation getting to know one another.

Richard was an airline pilot, and Jenny was a former model and now stay-at-home mom. As I began to share my love of time travel, ghosts, and all things haunted, they told me that they lived in what was once a monks' priory that was listed on the historic sites in England. It had a name—Cheswick Farm—and it was haunted. So much so that the media had featured it in the news, and it was being included in a book on haunting in Surrey, England.

It was one of those situations (for me, a blessing) where someone says to you: "If you're ever in my area, please feel free to come and stay as our guest at our haunted home," and, whether you are a psychic medium or not, you simply cannot resist the offer. And I am certainly one of those people who actually take other people at their word! There were so many things about taking such a trip that appealed to me. I really liked the Thomas family and welcomed the chance to know them better, and I had yet to travel overseas. I was extremely grateful and felt blessed for the opportunity to visit haunted England, all while staying in a haunted house under the guidance of people native to the country. I wanted to experience this very old, very haunted environment and didn't hesitate to accept the invitation. I said yes immediately.

The following year I was traveling alone on a Virgin Atlantic flight to Surrey, England.

Chapter Fourteen

CHESWICK FARM REIGATE/ SURREY, ENGLAND, 1990

··

AFTER A SEVEN-HOUR flight, my plane touched down in Gatwick Airport. The entire Thomas family met me in the airport lounge, and we stopped for a bite to eat on the way to Cheswick Farm. Jet lag took a while to take over, and I finally passed out in the backseat of the family car after leaving the quant pub we had lunched in. I crashed hard and didn't wake up until we arrived.

A large hedge flanked by two oak trees hid the house, and since I was visiting in June, spring never looked more beautiful. The lush greenery and full-flowered gardens were an awesome sight. What especially held me captive was the 230-year-old wisteria that bloomed so elegantly, it's scent a sweet fragrance of welcome.

The former home of Reigate priory monks, Cheswick is a sixteenth-century farmhouse that the Thomas family tenderly restored to breathtaking beauty. During the years of restoration, artifacts have been uncovered and mysteries revealed. Throughout the house are carved religious ornaments that blend Old World with New.

I loved the house and every story I was told about it. According to media coverage in 1982 and 1988, tales of Cheswick ghosts were common. Workers who were involved in the renovation would not stay there after dark, insisting they saw the monk in the front garden. Jenny had told me that the monk in a long tunic apparently haunted it. Whenever anyone speaks to him, he walks through the wall and disappears. As a child, Lia had seen him and called down to her mother, thinking it was one of the construction crew still in the house. It wasn't.

Other stories promised possible hauntings regarding the billiard room that was added in 1929. According to my journal at the time, I was told a "green swirl" had manifested itself in that room. No matter where I went on the property or in the house, I could "feel" the intensity of spirit and of other times. It is a breathtakingly beautiful place with lush green gardens surrounding the property and suites of rooms with rich wood and cozy fireplaces. Jenny once told me that you never knew what you might encounter from day to day—like the 1646 document they found during work on the two loft rooms. It had been there, untouched, for over three hundred years! The energy in Cheswick was electrifying and filled with the kind of ghost stories I wanted to experience. I remember speaking to my parents upon my arrival. After hearing some of the stories, my mother said: "Are you in the right place, or what?"

The Thomas family had four Yorkies they kept in the kitchen area. After some wet doggy kisses of hello, they showed me where I was staying.

My bedroom was an upper loft with a comfy bed, plush pillows, a dresser, and a vanity table. Two windows were flung open across from the bed and looked out toward the expanse of the property next door that had horses roaming free. I took a lot of photos from that window. The room I was in was referred to as the monk's room, and nailed to the wall beside the window was a very old, ornately carved image of a monk.

Over the two-week period in England, I had experiences that could pretty much cover a book of its own. For that reason, I have chosen to share only a few of them.

The Monk's Room

While the first night had me fall completely exhausted into the comfy, fluffy bed, it was the second night that had me anxious. I wasn't sure why, except for the fact that the anxiety felt very familiar and much like the masculine energy I had felt back when I was a student of William Hickey.

As I often do at night, and especially while on a trip, I opened my leather-bound journal and wrote about the day. The lamp was on low, and I was sitting propped up against two large pillows. It was late, long after eleven in the evening, and the house was asleep. As my eyelids grew heavier, I dropped the pen, moved the book to the night table, and snuggled into the billowy comforter, falling quickly to sleep. Maybe it was the country air or the fact that I felt safe in the room, as though being watched over by someone, but I was always completely rested when in the room.

I opened my eyes and read the numbers on my travel alarm clock: 4:44 a.m. I knew that was a numerological sign that angels surrounded me, and it was a reminder to me that I was never spiritually alone.

It was too late to go back to sleep and too early to get up, so I stayed in bed and put myself into a meditative space. I was breathing evenly and relaxed and not anticipating a thing, which is the time when the paranormal seems to trust the most. When we are in that state of relaxation of meditation and/or prayer, we raise our own vibration, and therefore we open ourselves to a deeper communication: a communication of energy.

It was during these deep breaths that I caught movement in the corner of my eye coming from the area of the vanity near the window. I slowly focused my eyes to become accustomed to the room and scanned from left to right. My eyes settled on the carving on the wall. I sat up a little and squinted at it. The room seemed to brighten, and the image of the monk appeared to move forward out of it and drew himself up to his full-length real height. That is the only way I can explain it. He manifested from that carving into a full-length man in shadow wearing a tunic, a hood, and sandals. He appeared to have walked out of the wall.

I remained perfectly still. My heart was beating rapidly, and I was scared. I wasn't sure if this was really happening. That's when I remembered that I had read and been told that if you spoke to the monk, he would disappear. At that moment I wasn't sure I wanted him to! We were at a stalemate, because neither of us was moving. I watched as the shadow figure eased in and out through the archway of the carving. I felt he wanted to say something to me. I decided to speak to him to test the theory.

As I opened my mouth to speak, he very slowly and deliberately walked through the wall, disappearing, to where I have not a clue. That was not the one and only time I saw the monk in my room. While staying there, I saw him at least two times: once in greeting and once, I believe, to say good-bye.

The Music & Billiard Room

Then came the night I was left alone in the house while the family ran errands and saw to personal commitments. I had changed into my pajamas, tossed on a robe, and made my way down the stairs to the kitchen to make some tea. While the kettle was on, I decided to investigate the part of the property that housed the addition, sometimes called the Music Room and, at one time, The Billiard Room. I remember going into the hallway with soft steps and sliding the latch bar up to push open the door to the room. I heard it creak and laughed at how scared I was. It is interesting how the darkness can play tricks on us and instill fear even when we are "in the light," so to speak.

I stepped into the room and jumped when the door closed behind me. It was dark except for my flashlight. I found the dimmer switch and turned on the light. I remember the family telling me stories of someone claiming to see a "green swirl" above the billiard table decades ago, perhaps in the 1930s. I stood still and moved the flashlight around the room. I was not in there more than five minutes when I caught movement by the smaller window panels directly across the room.

I centered the beam of light on the windows and squinted my eyes closed and then opened them again. Two green eyes stared back at me, and it felt menacing. I repeatedly moved the light around to see if the image was my imagination, but the eyes grew larger, as if they were trying to lead me out of the room. I wish I could say that I faced whatever this was straight on and did something about it, but that is far from what I actually did. I was not as experienced with negativity as I am now, and my instinct was to hightail it out of that room, which I did and with great speed. I remember lifting and closing the bar and latch, crossing the hallway toward the kitchen to cancel my tea, and nearly tripping on my way up the stairs to the safety of my bed with the monk. It was the lesser of two evils in my mind.

Tower of London

One of our trips took us to the Tower of London. Richard, Lia, and I took to the Underground into the city. It seemed so much cleaner than the Subway in New York City. We took in the sites, rode the trolley and the train, and shopped till we dropped at Harrods and Piccadilly before going up to the Tower itself. I was younger, but those winding stairs were incredible to climb. I recall at one point standing near the armor of Henry VIII and feeling a chill grip me.

"What is that?" I asked aloud.

"What?" It was Lia who spoke. "What do you hear?"

"Screams. I'm hearing yelling and screaming."

Her eyes widened. "Look down."

At my feet, exactly where I was standing, was a plaque. It read: "17 July 1974, a bomb placed here exploded killing one and injuring thirty-five others."

Chapter Fifteen

GETTYSBURG, 1994

····································

IN 1993 THE miniseries *Gettysburg* appeared to great acclaim on televisions across the nation. It played out the three bloody days of the battle of Gettysburg and interested many people to take a trip to see the battlefields, especially considering the fact that they were at this time under threat regarding preservation. From that point of view alone, I wanted to visit, and I was desperately focused on saving historic sites for future generations to know about and explore.

This was another one of those trips that I took with my friend Nina. This time it was during the exact days of the battle in July when the heat was the most oppressive. I felt it was extremely important to go on the days and month the battle actually took place if we wanted to experience anything paranormal. That would be when the energy would be strongest for the life-changing events that had taken place all those many years ago. So we made reservations for the Farnsworth House, which was authentic to the Civil War, for July 1 through July 8. It helped that its facade was riddled with bullet holes and that they offered ghost tours of the house, the basement, and the surrounding Gettysburg College campus, and all of them had tales of being haunted.

The first day, we arrived at our destination earlier than planned, and the moment we hit town, I had an insane focus to get to the Visitor Center.

"Why are you in such a rush to go there now?" Nina asked.

We were both tired from the ride. It had been one detour after another, and I felt like I was being prevented, yet encouraged to go there. It was like someone was putting the obstacles in my way on purpose, but I remained cool and focused—almost driven.

"Here it is." I pulled into a parking spot. As Nina went to find a ladies room, I found myself walking around the place like I had been there before, and I walked straight up to a special window showcase. I stood there for several long minutes staring at the contents on display in this one particular panel. I scanned it and slowly sat down on my knees to see the bottommost part of the window.

"Found on the body of a soldier on Seminary Ridge."

The contents were several good luck stones, a button, and what caught my eye and meant the most to me, a single quartz crystal point.

"What are you looking at?" Nina was on her knees beside me, staring into the window.

"I'm fascinated by what was found on this soldier's body. He has a clear quartz crystal!"

Nina frowned. "Fat lot of good it did him."

I grimaced and stood up. "Not sure why I was led here, but I was directed to this spot to see this crystal."

At check-in, we were early enough to be able to meet the proprietor of the house. We were shown into our room, which had twin beds, and the bathroom was unfortunately down the hall. But we were grateful we didn't have to share it with other guests.

After unpacking and a dinner out in the patio café next door, we planned the week ahead. That would include a guideless (we didn't want to be rushed) auto tour via cassette tape, some ghost hunting at the inn, the ghost tour, and walking the battlefields. The battlefields alone would constitute a single trip unto itself. We were not sure what we could see in one day and promised we wouldn't adhere too close to a schedule. After all, this was supposed to be a vacation, and while being the tourist is fun, it can be tiring and draining. We fit relaxation time into the mix, and I was going to bed on the earlier side so we could start the first day off before the crowds. Plus, I was looking forward to the continental breakfast on the outdoor patio!

* * *

Ping! It was faint at first, so faint I almost didn't hear it at all.

Ping! Ping!

I stirred and then turned over. In those moments the pinging continued, and I soon felt a hand slowly and lightly slide down my right cheek. I jumped out of the bed as if scorched and stood staring at it. I was too stunned to turn on the light because I had been in a sound sleep, and the unexpectedness was overwhelming.

After a few moments, I "came to," as it were, and once again tuned into the sound. I turned to the source, the window facing the side street. The light was streaming in from the streetlamp, and it lit a path to the pillow I had been sleeping on. I followed the trail with my eyes and then I heard, and *saw*, the sound.

Ping! Pebbles. Tiny stones were hitting the glass of the windowpanes and bouncing off. This is where the paranormal investigator in me strove to separate fact from fiction. Maybe this wasn't a ghostly situation at all. Maybe I had dreamed the hand on my cheek, and a real person was actually down below. Perhaps he or she had mistaken my room for someone else's. I walked to the window, pulled back the thin lace curtains, and looked down at the street below. No one. I scanned to the right and left. The street was empty. I turned away from the window and started to walk back to the bed.

Ping!

I swung around and made quick steps back to the window. The little stones kept hitting it, but no one was on the street! This was unnerving because I wasn't prepared for it. It would be several years before I would be comfortable enough to recognize what I could handle and what I could not, in terms of the paranormal. So, I did what most people would do: I ran out of that room and roused Nina from slumber to share the story. I was shaking her violently, and she was clueless as to my panic. As far as I was concerned, daylight could not come quick enough, and I was looking forward to seeing what more might be in store. We spent the remainder of the night talking about it because I refused to go back to my room. When she finally fell asleep, I curled up on the sofa and wrote about the experience in my travel journal.

The Ghost Walking Tour to Gettysburg College Campus

The next day was spent touring the battlefields and, as is custom in historic places, you will find people dressed as docents and re-enactors of the era. It makes it difficult for someone to determine whether they are seeing an actor or a ghost. Then, again, that is part of the allure, and it's a welcomed part because history is amazing when one walks in the steps of those who blazed trails before us and *for* us.

After dinner we took the Ghost Walking Tour with the ten other guests who signed up for what was promised to be a real scary excursion. A young man dressed in costume took us by lantern light through the streets, pointing out haunted houses while delighting in sharing ghost stories. Nina found him refreshing because he was so into it that his exuberance was infectious. However, that same exuberance was making me nervous, and we moved to the back to pick up the rear and waited for the right opportunity to break away from the group. Soon, we arrived at the campus of Gettysburg College, where our guide entertained us with a story of lovers plunging to their deaths in a suicide pact from the roof, and another about a ghost child writing the word "Help" on a window. The more he talked, the darker his stories became, and I couldn't find an "exit" bench fast enough to escape them. He was a little too good at his descriptions, it was really late, and I could get a strong sense of denseness in the air. It was as if the entire area was thick with fog, yet we could all see clearly. I also couldn't shake the strong scent of horse manure. We sat quietly on the bench, and I took out my high-powered flashlight.

"You'll scare away the ghosts," Nina said.

"No way; it's not the dead I'm afraid of," I answered. "But it may certainly scare away any *live* people who might be roaming around, which is how it can be helpful."

We sighed in unison. I switched on the flashlight, and we moved away from the bench. The night was warm, with not much of a breeze, and we were sitting right below the beautifully crafted clock tower, still embraced by the odor of horse manure.

"Not so beautiful when you think about that couple jumping to their deaths."

The ray of sunshine had spoken. Nina always had a way of putting things in blunt perspective in all situations. I didn't answer as we blazed a path with my flashlight around the campus grounds. We walked in silence a while and at one point heard a rustle in the trees behind us. Rather than look there, we looked at each other.

"Please don't tell me you're going to turn around."

"Stay here."

"No way!"

We both turned, and I switched on the light and focused it on where we heard the rustling. In the distance was a man dressed in the uniform of a Union soldier. The light swinging from his hand was not a flashlight, but a lantern. Nina had completely disappeared from my view as I watched him. First, I thought he was a re-enactor who was still on the job. There were so many around dressed in costumes that one got used to seeing them walking around. However, this man was different. Young, solemn, he had eyes far more expressive than those I had ever encountered. They were very dark, moody, and watery, as if they had been tearing. And I read pain in them. Not physical pain, but the pain from lack of recognition on my part.

I approached him, he turned, and it was then that I became aware of the fact that he appeared to be missing an arm, or at least I thought he was missing an arm. I wasn't sure from my vantage point. I watched him walk away and disappear behind a nearby tree. I waited, not sure what I was waiting for, but that soldier never came out from the other side of that tree. He simply disappeared.

A tiny gasp escaped from my lips, and I turned to Nina, my heart racing wildly.

"What did you see?" Nina was already walking ahead of me and toward the campus exit.

"A ghost," I answered, catching up beside her. "I saw a ghost. I wonder who he was?" We continued our escape. "Major." I whispered the name, but he was long gone, and so was Nina, who was already running ahead.

Historic Cheswick Farmhouse

Bomb Plaque

Major's Crystal

Chapter Sixteen

MOVING RIGHT ALONG

....

READING PEOPLE BECAME a social outlet for me, and I enjoyed making new friends and traveling to different events. The people I read insisted on paying me "something," and one co-worker/friend reasoned that many of them would spend at least twenty-five dollars in a bar for cocktails, so twenty-five dollars for a reading plus food and drink in the privacy of her house was a bargain.

She invited about ten people for Friday night pizza with the girls. The law of attraction was working in my favor, because each pizza night a different woman would invite me to her home for a future psychic pizza party of her own. It forced me to make a quick run to the store to buy a calendar, which I promptly nailed to the front of my closet door near the kitchen that was my "home office."

And while we are on the topic of pizza, there were many times when I would go on shopping sprees with friends and/or family and a reading was exchanged for our dinners.

I unintentionally began to build a following among the clients of the attorneys I was working for. Around 1995, I was working part-time for a law firm in Caldwell, NJ, about twenty minutes from home, to supplement my writing income. One afternoon I came in early to go over the pile of cases one of the attorneys had for the week. As we went through the files together, I would read the name of the client with some general information while she noted it on her calendar in order to prepare for the case. I remember looking down at one of the names and shaking my head.

"This person is so dishonest. He is abusive to his wife, and he is in debt. I doubt he could even pay your bill." I looked up at the astonished attorney.

"Linda, why would you say that? Do you know him?"

I shook my head. I had no facts or knowledge to back up what I was saying. The man was a stranger to me, as the attorney had yet to even take him on as a client. All I knew was that when I looked down at his handwriting and saw his signature, I was overwhelmed with information and felt compelled to share it. The attorney tossed another file to me, this time with clients I didn't know but whom she knew well enough. I read the handwriting and signatures of each. Soon, we were joined by two of the other partners in the law firm with files of their own for me to read. From what they confirmed, I was 90 percent accurate. Before I knew it, my part-time job description with them changed, and I was now "reading" or intuiting the work in their case files on a regular basis.

It wasn't long before I felt the need to unleash all that energy and embrace working as a psychic full-time.

Talk about leaping empty-handed into the void. I left a secure, highly paid position and stopped freelance writing, with no other place to go and only a small following to depend on to pay the bills.

It's common knowledge among my peers that when one starts out in this business, a practical way to build a following is to be open to doing psychic parties. Psychic "parties" are usually readings of about eight to ten people at someone's home. The host or hostess of these parties usually invites friends who are interested in getting a reading to come to their home to have refreshments, snacks, or sometimes even a buffet lunch or dinner as part of the event. The psychic is considered the "entertainment." These visits are always good venues for networking opportunities and a great way to meet new people and embrace new friendships, not to mention hone my skills regarding these abilities that I was becoming more familiar with.

Depending upon the psychic, a party can consist of readings anywhere from fifteen minutes to a half hour and usually takes place in the dining room, bedroom, or den of the person who is hosting. Every house lends itself to a different setup. For some psychics, they are fine with working with the energy of someone else's home. For me, the energy in each house is so different that it isn't always conducive, or even comfortable, to have serious readings.

These "parties" were mostly for entertainment purposes, which meant that alcohol was served and the atmosphere was more "party" than "spiritual." That did not make my job any easier, because for me to read these people, I would have to remind the host to tell the guests to not drink alcohol until after their reading, because it changes their energy and can make for a challenging reading for both of us. For the last person on the list, that could be two hours away, and my request wasn't always adhered to. Eventually, by the end of the "party," I would find myself sitting across an extremely inebriated individual whose energy was so skewered by their alcohol intake that they missed out on what could have been a helpful reading because they couldn't really connect to the situation.

My first psychic party was for Dana, the client I had appeared in court on behalf of during her divorce. Dana lived in a brand new million-dollar home she acquired from her ex-husband. She was a very pretty and popular woman in her thirties with two teenage daughters, both under her roof. She arranged for them to be at the movies on a Friday night, and invited about eight of her friends to the house. Mom came with me to field personal questions about me, which inevitably come up when I am in a group of any kind. It is common curiosity to want to know how I came to do what I do, what my life is like, or what experiences I have had.

While I attended to the readings, Mom would be where the action was with those who were waiting, regaling them with stories of me as a child. Her help was invaluable because it allowed me to focus all my energies on the readings.

Dana had a beautifully finished basement that was like a mini-apartment, complete with living room, dining room, kitchen and pull-out sofa bed. I set myself up at the round mahogany dining room table and waited for the first client to come down for her reading.

The first person was an attractive woman in her mid-thirties, whom we'll call "Teri" for purposes of this book. I was using Tarot cards at the time as a catalyst for each reading session, because it helped me focus on the colors coming out of the person's mouths rather than to stare at them. It also seemed to make the client feel they were getting something more, because cards were involved. (Eventually, I created my own color and energy deck to use for when I needed to zone intensely on what was coming from my client and wanted to maintain that focus.)

I remember turning a few cards over and looking up at Teri for validation. I found myself staring into her eyes, not able to physically look away, nor did I feel I wanted to. Fortunately, Teri was the kind of person who went with the flow of things, which allowed me to "read" her in a more penetrating light. I found myself squaring off her right eye, and, like a television screen, I began to see images. First they were in black-and-white, but they soon became more colorful and more clearly defined. It wasn't until much later that I realized these pictures or movies were a form of clairvoyance.

I began talking to her in a monotone, suggesting information that I had no way of knowing previous to our meeting. I "saw" Teri giving birth to a daughter only a few months prior, as well as a new house, which I described as white with a very long driveway and a full wraparound porch on the second level. As this zoning out continued, an image began to materialize and super-impose itself over Teri's face. The image was of a woman who looked remarkably like her, only the hair was tighter in curls and blonder, the face older.

Teri's hand flew to her mouth, and tears sprang to her eyes. "That's my mother!" Her words were like an intrusion and snapped me quickly out of the zone or trance I was in. Teri continued to validate what I was seeing by telling me that, yes, she had given birth to a baby girl recently, and she and her husband had purchased the exact house I described. Later that evening, as she shared her experience with the others, she asked me if I would come for a psychic party at her house, adding, "You should have no trouble finding the house, seeing that you have already been there!"

Chapter Seventeen

READ ME! READ ME!

·······································

THAT NIGHT AND that first psychic party changed everything for me. A demand for me to do parties started coming from unlikely people. I was hired by Volkswagen, among other businesses, to do their corporate parties with private events at swanky underground nightclubs and establishments like Tavern on the Green. My hire was always word of mouth, and the guest lists were dotted with celebrities, politicians, and representatives from other corporations. I was thriving in this new environment, and within six months I found myself working in a New Age center in the next town.

Everyone has their own idea of how they want to create their spirit and what beliefs they want to be known for having. One thing that was and is constant for me is that I am Christian, and I live in the light of God. The spirit I embrace is a divine one where angels and guides share rituals of meditation and prayer. Though I am not "New Age" and I am not "occult," the metaphysical center I had just started working at, was. I was the only mainstream thing about the place, and

I had to prove myself to the town in order to build a following.

"How do you propose to do that?" the owner asked me when I first walked in his establishment. "Anyone working here is in charge of their own publicity, and there isn't much time for an ad to introduce you this week."

I wasn't concerned. I had surrendered the issue of this work to God and knew that my angels and guides, His messengers, were going to make sure that this work would be an effortless endeavor. My faith had sustained me this far.

"Why don't we advertise free sixty-second readings? People love to get something free. I know I do."

The owner created a sandwich board sign and put it out on the sidewalk in front of his shop. A nice little line started to form around noon that day. As each person came up to me, I took their hand and stared into their eyes. Despite the fact that it could be draining, I enjoyed Zoning and knew that the more I did it, the more I was honing that ability.

As one o'clock rolled around, the word had gotten out round the neighborhood, and the line was literally forming out of the store and down the street to the right. Not only was I becoming known in the area, but also I was developing a following of people who were making appointments for future readings. The appointment book was filling up, and faith was now allowing me to make a living as a psychic.

I was booking appointments at his establishment six days a week, with Sunday off. My promise to God and myself was to not read on a Sunday and to use that day as a day of gratitude.

When I wasn't working there, I usually hung out with the owner and my new psychic friends. He had introduced me to the others in the area, and on his payroll and we would often spend long candlelit hours, sometimes until 4:00 or 5:00 a.m. the next day, in the back room, giving each other readings. I know it sounds strange, but when psychics get together, they like to trade readings as a way to unwind. We were polishing our skills and coming up with some pretty emotionally revealing information. Contrary to popular belief, more men are working psychics than women. Most nights I was the only female in the group, aside from an occasional visit from the women who owned a shop down the street.

The "back room" was the Reading Room that the psychics and astrologers at the center shared to see clients. It was a decent size, had its own private entrance from the rear of the parking lot, and had its own private bathroom. Glass sliding doors separated it from the rest of the facility, with a curtain partially draped over one side for privacy. Lovingly provided by the owner's handy grandfather were two cubbyholes on either side of the doors that acted as shelves for candles or figurines. An oblong table with two chairs was the centerpiece of the room; behind it, a comfy sofa. Candles completed the picture, and it was here that I spent most of my time.

The busier and more in demand I became, the more important it was to go within to seek that mindfulness connection with my higher self. I had quickly found that my rediscovery of meditation was also affording me communication with a more divine connection.

One of my most powerful meditative experiences came after a late night of a back-to-back reading schedule and some friendly back room readings to unwind. The first thing I did when I got home was to take a quick shower, slip into my pajamas, and meditate before bed. I had a cane rocker at the end of my bed, and I sat in it to establish my daily meditative connections. I quickly learned that the benefits of mindful meditation—the act of "going within"—to communicate and reason, had no limits. By embracing this simple act of breathing, I was able to reason rather than react, and that was going to come in handy in life no matter what one did for a living.

My lavender robe warmly wrapped around me, I arranged Mom's hand-crocheted blanket over my knees and inhaled a deep breath before putting the chair into a gentle rocking motion. It was dark except for a night-light in the kitchen. A large white pillar candle on the nearby coffee table illuminated the room, and even though my eyes were closed, I could "see" the flame dancing in front of me.

It took a few minutes for me to get into a meditative state, and I eventually realized I was breathing steadily, eyes closed, and I was extremely calm and centered. I was not alone in the room, and that realization manifested itself very slowly, until I sensed a shadow pass in front of my closed lids. I kept them closed, and the shadow shifted, and it became more clearly defined as a woman—a very familiar woman.

"Aunt Jenny?" I asked, my voice floating in the darkness as I squeezed my eyes tighter, afraid to open them. She had died only recently, and I had often visited her with my mother and grandmother for lunch when she was alive.

Her face went from a shadow to a cameo and, finally, the face of the woman I knew. I could also see her hands come into view, and they were moving wildly. She was definitely trying to get my attention.

Then, without further warning, she disappeared just as slowly. I sat there for a long time contemplating what had just happened before logging the experience in my journal and retiring for the night. I embraced this way of connecting with spirit and looked forward to each and every meditation, hoping for the same results. I was rarely disappointed.

Chapter Eighteen

THE EARLY READINGS

....

I FELT SO BLESSED to meet each and every person and would often arrive at the New Age shop a little earlier to meditate and center myself. Twice a week I knew that at one o'clock a sweet, elderly woman in her late eighties would be stopping by to see me. She lived in the area and often walked to the nearby bodega to pick up her newspaper, because this is how she got her exercise. A visit to me was usually her next stop. She made sure to always have an appointment booked, and she would arrive with a sack filled with photos in albums and others loose or in envelopes. Every picture was labeled with the year, place/event, and the people in the photo.

"My family thinks I'm too old to bother with now, so they don't want to hear my stories." She sat down in the chair to the left of me (she would never sit across, because it was easier for her to show me her photos) and placed one of the albums carefully on the reading table. "I'm so happy you are here to talk to and assure me." She smiled.

I went over to the water cooler and poured some hot water into two cups for the tea she insisted we have together. I liked her a lot, and my heart ached for the fact that she wanted desperately to share her stories, family history, and money with her grown children and grandchildren. They were interested in the money, but not her or anything about her, so one day she told them that they couldn't inherit any money because she didn't have it. It wasn't long before they stopped visiting and calling, finally disappearing from her life. But she did have a great deal of money and said she had been testing them. You see, she had sold her life story to Hollywood back in the day, and she said it became the movie with Tallulah Bankhead. Her husband had invested the money for her, and she was going to be able to live out her life in whatever style she saw fit. Unfortunately, that would be without family, but she had a nice, clean little house and was in good health. Her intention was to enjoy each day, and she would be leaving her money to a charity for survivors of shipwrecks.

The photographs inside the book were mounted to little black corner tabs that she had glued onto the page. The book itself was big and black, and the handwriting was a flowery flourish of penmanship. I would settle in and look at each photo as she told her stories and we sipped tea. She was so slight to sit next to, and I could feel a warmth and a loving vibration coming from her when she spoke. There were times she would stop and ask me to tune in to the photo and tell her how it made me feel and what I "saw" that was not there. I began to really sense the emotions in vibration because of these photograph sessions, and I soon became adept at "reading" photos because of my time with her. And I never charged her after her first visit. I enjoyed her company as much as she said she enjoyed mine! I'm sure that the chances of her being alive now, some twenty years later, are not that great. But I have thought of her often, and I am grateful for the guidance she so freely gave me. She was an inspiration.

It was during this time that I started writing novels, with a particular focus on time travel romance and ghost stories. *Fate Magazine* played a substantial part in this because I wrote true ghost stories for them in that section of the magazine. I soon worked my way to other magazines, freelancing various articles and short stories on everything from angels and astrology to psychic awareness and zoning, and was pleased to be adding income as a writer to my résumé.

One day, I had the interesting fortune to meet my first real Gypsy when a very robust, heavy-set woman came into the shop. She walked with a cane and was accompanied by two dark-haired young men in their twenties who she introduced as her grandsons, "the twins." The owner of the shop seemed to know who she was, as he respectfully grabbed an empty chair from behind the cash register so that she could sit down.

"I have come for good reason," she said, getting straight to the point. "Where is this psychic I hear about?" she asked, her eyes directed at me. "Is it you?" She sat down in the chair and folded her arms across her chest. "I want you should look into my eyes," she said in her thick accent.

I came closer and took her hand into mine as the owner slid another chair over for me to sit in. "Try to maintain focus," I said to prepare her for my zoning. "It's okay for you to blink; just relax."

The images flashed quickly the moment I squared off her eye: a brown box with the initial *B* carved into it, something green, like money, was inside. The box was on a shelf in the closet of an old house. Then I "saw" a dollar amount and repeated the number thirty-five thousand dollars out loud.

"I must have reading *now!*" she demanded while jumping up and breaking eye contact. The two young men rushed to her side. "No, you wait out here."

We went into the reading room in the back of the shop, safe from being heard behind a glass sliding door, and safe from being seen, as that door was covered by a drape. I was sure we were not alone—that the person who was letting me "see" this box and money was doing so deliberately. I told her this, and she seemed quite satisfied.

"Yes, it is him. The '*B*' stands for Barry. He owns box," she explained in fractured English. "Barry is dead. He left some cash for me, but we can't find it. Where do you see box? In his house?"

"I'm not sure," I answered honestly. "I feel as if it's in a closet on a top shelf. I'm not getting much more than that."

She leaned forward and patted my hand. "You done good." She got up and walked back to the front of the shop, motioning to the twins with a nod to the door. "We let you know, eh?" And she was gone.

About a week later, we received a call from one of the twins telling us that their grandmother had found the cash. It was exactly where I had said it would be, on the top shelf of one of Barry's closets. The amount he left her turned out to be thirty-five thousand dollars. Did I get a finder's fee? No such luck. But at least Barry is resting in peace.

Deborah the Dancer was an interesting find in a client. A flight attendant friend who booked readings with me regularly had referred her. Opportunities to dance were being offered her in film and on television, and she was turning them down if it involved air travel, because her friend said she was terrified to fly. A short, petite brunette, she was a twenty-seven-year-old professional dancer. She was sweet and personable, and I liked Deborah immediately. She lived in Manhattan and danced especially to please her spirit. I found her to be inspiring, and that inspiration was apparently mutually felt, because she began to schedule regular sessions with me.

I have a policy of not letting someone see me too soon between readings unless they are coming on an issue unrelated to their last session. I rarely will "read" the same issue if clients have made no attempt to help themselves in the situation. I have seen too many people become psychic dependent, relying only on outside guidance rather than incorporating it with his or her own. It's important to remember that we all have our own personal power called intuition. That intuition, when listened to, will right things for us in many areas of our lives. I enjoy opening that door for people, but my first challenge with Deborah was to help her with her insecurity of flying on an airplane.

She had rationalized the situation this way: if she knew ahead of time that the flight would be okay, then she would feel better about going. She booked readings before every holiday and summer vacation, and she always called me at the last possible minute, when she knew I couldn't refuse her.

"There's a delay on the plane!" She was in a panic.

It had been a long day of readings, and I was leaving for the night when I got her call. "Are you okay?"

That year she was hired for Italian TV and would have to travel to Italy. She was not only nervous about the long flight but also obsessed with the fact that she didn't know the language. During her reading, which took place at the last minute while she was about to take off, the number four kept flashing in my mind. I proceeded to tell her that she would not have to worry about anything because the number four was going to save the day for her.

Keeping that in mind, Deborah took her trip to Italy and stayed three weeks. She phoned me with an update after she settled in Rome at the end of the first day.

"Linda, the number four has been everywhere!" she confirmed excitedly. "When I arrived, there were no taxis, but the fourth person stopped and offered me a ride directly to the front door of my hotel. His car had the number four-one-four in the license, and my hotel room was number forty-four! I am so relieved." I was glad for Deborah, but exhausted from the in-flight reading!

When Deborah returned home, she referred a new client to me, a high-maintenance divorcée named Dalya. She arrived for her appointment at the shop dressed in seven-inch spiked heels, a tight pair of black slacks, a white silk blouse that accentuated her tan, and a large white picture hat. Her hair was as white as her blouse, and she became the catalyst for me asking clients not to wear any perfume or cologne when they came for their readings, as you could smell Dalya before she even hit the door of the shop. She introduced herself and sat in the chair across from me.

"I want to know about my love life," she said.

(I have always defined the issues of clients as "ance-y"—romance and finance seem to be the main issues people want to know about in a reading.)

I started the reading with my trusty, rapidly aging tarot deck, slowly flipping over each card, while addressing the issue of money. Fifteen minutes into the reading, I felt an overwhelming feeling of love being directed at her, but through me. I looked up from my card flipping and smiled.

"Malcolm is going to be very interested in taking that trip to Florida with you soon," I said. "There will be a—"

"What?" she screamed, cutting me off. "*Malcolm?* Did you just say 'Malcolm'? I didn't say Malcolm. Did I say Malcolm?" She rattled on excitedly. "I never said his name was Malcolm! How do you know his name is Malcolm?"

"I'm psychic," I answered.

"That's amazing." She leaned back in her chair and laughed.

* * *

In the six brief months of my affiliation with this store/center, I had met enough people to go off on my own, especially due to the flurry of psychic validations that I had testimony for on a daily basis. The incidents of testimony often happened while the people were still being read, as many were able to validate things I had said almost immediately.

Chapter Nineteen

MANY SPIRITS, MANY VISITS—MY FIRST OFFICE

· ·

I WANTED TO CONTINUE to bring psychic work mainstream, and that would mean setting up in a proper office space, not in a New Age shop. November 30 was my last day at the New Age center. It was also my mom's birthday, and we celebrated by having dinner together. She was very proud of the way things were unfolding for me, and together we were embracing a new spiritual way that drew us even closer together, if that were possible. Some knew Mom as "psychic mom" and also "the dream lady," to those she would interpret dreams for. Unlike my career, she dispensed her advice and interpretation for free, and when she felt like it. She didn't go into business or hang a shingle, and only family and friends were aware of her talent.

Despite the fact that Mom was helping me with some of the paperwork of the business, I kept my own calendar and made all my appointments personally. I was determined to have an office so that next year's tax return legally placed me as a Psychic Consultant. Mom and I put it out there, so to speak, through prayer and strong intention. One evening, while on our way to one of these psychic parties, we passed a For Rent sign at an office building about a mile up the road from my house. Having some time to spare, we parked and rang the landlord's bell. He was an attorney who had known some of the people I had worked for, and as it turned out, he had three office spaces available to choose from for January 1. Further, if we liked one of them, we could move in the last week of December.

As the landlord escorted us up the stairs to the offices, I felt a strong pull to one particular office suite. He opened the door to an outer office, which was a reception area, and inside that were three other offices, one already occupied by another attorney. According to the landlord, the attorney in residence only used the place a couple of days a week, so I would be assured to have the entire third floor to myself the majority of the time. What was further attractive was the fact that I had available to me a free waiting room and a private entrance for my clients to use at the back of the building.

A special bonus to Mom was the fact that the building had an alarm system that centrally called to the police station in the event of intruders, and I would be safe there if I needed to be alone. As we continued our conversation, I was immediately drawn to an office door. When the landlord opened it, I understood why. The office was laid out in a very unusual placement of energy. When you opened the door, there was an expansive space, and further in, right in the middle of the room in front of one of the two windows, was an alcove that would fit a large, circular table and two chairs perfectly.

On December 28, with the help of a friend, I moved in my now-late-uncle's antique octagon-shaped mahogany table, two chairs from my grandmother, a small antique mahogany dressing table to use as a sacred space, and a desk, compliments of the landlord. As an office-warming gift, Mom and Dad bought me a mauve and white wicker loveseat with matching end tables. It all felt right. I was officially in business and could start booking my first clients in the new office.

Once the room was set up, Mom wanted to give it her blessings, and the once-over, before I started seeing clients. That Saturday evening we drove there with a coffeemaker and three gold-painted angel statues playing instruments. The trio had belonged to my Aunt Dolly, Mom's sister who had recently passed away.

Having set up the coffeemaker, I placed the three angels across the desk.

"I'll be sitting in the waiting room if you need me," Mom said.

Each angel figure depicted playing an instrument: two horns and one violin. I placed the angel with the violin in the center, but in looking at it now, I saw that it was missing the bow. I put my keys down on the desk and retrieved an incense stick from the top drawer. It made for a perfect bow. Dusting off my hands, I took a step back and took in the "look" of the office. Pleased with the results, I turned out the light, slid the doorknob to the lock position, and was closing the door behind me while simultaneously "seeing" the keys on top of the desk, still inside the room!

Aware of what I'd just done, Mom groaned aloud. "I can't believe you just did that!" She shook her head, "We have no spare, Linda, and we are locked in from the inside and we are locked out from the inside office. Try your cell phone."

Flipping open my cell phone, I paced the office, vainly trying to get a signal. Failing miserably, I turned to Mom. "We're in a dead zone, and I can't get a signal. Who would I call anyway? I have no number for the landlord, and it's Saturday, Mom, so no one is going to be coming to the building for me to get help from."

Tears sprang to Mom's eyes. "Well, what are we going to do, Linda?"

I stopped in mid-pace. "We're going to start praying, Mom. We both pontificate about the power of prayer; well, now is as good a time as any to have faith."

I kept going over to the doorknob and jiggling it to no avail. I spoke out loud. "Angels, please, please help us. No one will be here until Monday, and though we have a bathroom here, we don't want to spend the weekend up here like this. Please help."

"Please help us, Angels," I heard Mom say sweetly from behind me. "Please open the door for us." I turned to Mom and smiled. Together we said a prayer. I went over to the door again and gave it a turn.

"Angels, open for us," I said one more time as I could feel Mom's energy panic. I put my hand on the knob once more and turned. Nothing. I moved back from the door and watched as we both heard a click and saw the door softly swing open. As it did, the tears in my eyes began to spill down to my cheeks. "Thank you, thank you, thank you."

I turned around and saw that Mom was shaking her head while both crying and laughing at the same time. It was at that single moment that we were aware that we were not alone, that our angels and guides were watching over us.

"You make damn sure you have a duplicate set of keys in your purse for emergency. This can't happen again."

I nodded, relieved to be able to leave the panic of being locked inside the building. "Yes, first thing. I promise."

But, as we would soon discover, their "help" didn't stop there. As we got safely into the car and headed for home, I had an insane desire to rent a movie and headed for our local strip mall to see the latest releases.

"I won't be long," I said as I pulled into the parking space in front of the video store. "Do you want anything while I'm in there?"

"No. You go ahead. I've had enough excitement for one night."

I laughed and quickly ran into the store. I can't recall now what the movie was that I rented, but I do remember standing in line and hearing a "whirring" sound accompanied by jingling when I finally arrived at the checkout counter. The whirring sound got louder and louder.

"If I didn't know better, I'd think I was hearing a key-making machine," I said to the cashier who was ringing up my order.

"Yes. We make keys."

I smiled at him and looked up and quietly said, "Thank you, Angels…"

"You are welcome," the cashier said as he took the key from me to duplicate. "But how did you know my name?"

I was extremely confused. "What do you mean?"

"You said to me, thank you, Angel." He smiled again. "That's me!"

"Your name is Angel?" I asked, incredulous.

"Yes, and you are most welcome."

I left the store with my movie, duplicate key, and genuine warmth in my heart for the "angels" that walk on Earth!

Chapter Twenty

MY CIVIC DUTY, JUST DON'T TELL ANYONE

....

THOUGH WE ARE not always publicly acknowledged for our help in cases at the request of law enforcement, psychics are often called upon to perform the valuable service of finding missing persons.

Word of my clairvoyance reached the ears of some people in my local law enforcement, and I was asked to "zone in" on a map to locate missing children. That entire event is a blur because it happened in such a rush. I can recall that I was still working at the New Age center at the time. Two plainclothes policemen came in and asked, off the cuff, if I would look at a map. They had "heard" of me.

They spent about a half an hour in the back room and spread two maps out on the table: one was of the United States, and the other was more local to the area of where they were looking for missing persons.

"This case goes back," explained the taller of the two as he pulled out a chair and sat at the reading table. His partner pulled the chair out next to him. "Is there anything at all you can pick up? We hear that's sometimes possible."

Both men darted questionable looks to each other and then returned a hopeful smile to me.

Let me say here that I was never very good at reading maps but always had a good sense of direction if I needed one. The maps in front of me meant nothing, and I was at a loss as to how to go about tuning into them for the sake of locating a missing person.

Mistaking my hesitation for insecure reluctance, the second officer looked up. "Anything. Just give us anything. We won't hold you to it." He took a pen from his pocket and used it as a pointer. "The group of children was on a camping trip with their pastor and his assistant, and the last time they were all seen was in this area." He tapped his pen on the map.

I looked down. He was pointing to Rockaway Township, but that didn't feel right. "When?" I asked as I sat down to investigate further.

"Well, that's the thing," the other man said. "It's a cold case that goes back about twenty years. We saw the sign, heard about you, and decided to come in."

"He means it's not an active case, but it's one that we'd like to solve." His partner smiled.

I looked back down at the map, and my vision blurred and cleared up like a daydream. I zoned in, and I began to see a red bull's-eye form around the name of a town. Again, red was warning me about something, and I suddenly felt desperately sad.

"Here." I pointed to the word *Newark*. The other man reached over with an actual red marker and circled the area I had indicated.

"Why?"

"I'm seeing liquid vats and large buildings. I don't know what the place is, but I don't sense that it's operational anymore." I pushed the map forward and looked up at them. "I wish I could help you, but that is all I'm getting."

They got up, extended hands, and thanked me for my time while leaving a generous tip that I donated to the center for supplies.

One night I got a call from one of the detectives to thank me for my help. They had located the missing remains of the children in the area of the old Budweiser Brewery that had long since been abandoned. Those were the vats he said I "saw" when I pointed to the map.

I worked for various people regarding missing persons, and the routine was always the same. The official would give me sketchy details on the case, and we often visited the area where the missing person was last seen. I would zone in on a map or take an article of clothing belonging to the missing person and derive information through that exchange of energy. These experiences were draining and depressing, as often we were too late to find them, and those missing persons quickly became victims. Those cases stayed with me for a long time after. I found it too difficult to continue this aspect of the work.

One case that was brought to my attention had been investigated by *Unsolved Mysteries*, the popular TV show, regarding a missing reporter for the *Village Voice* named Susan Walsh. After meeting Susan Walsh's mother at one of my lectures, she hired me to also work on the case. Below is the report I filed for Martha Young at the Nutley Police Department. Note that many psychics have worked on this case, and my understanding of what happened is my own intuitive assessment, made back in 1997.

The Susan Walsh Case

Psychic Assessment by Linda Lauren—Case #8147
Assisted by Frances Gialanella
Disappearance of Susan Walsh
Dated: October 19, 1997

On August 14, 1997, Martha Young, the mother of Susan Walsh, approached me while I was lecturing at Barnes & Noble Bookstore in West Patterson, New Jersey. She requested my assistance in working to find any missing pieces to the puzzling disappearance of her daughter, which occurred last July, 1996, and whose story garnished a lot of media attention.

On August 19, 1997, accompanied by Frances Gialanella, we visited the home of Martha Young in Wayne, New Jersey. To that end, we looked at various newspaper articles, listened to a radio interview that discussed her life, and watched VCR tapes of Susan Walsh on *The Jerry Springer*

Show, reports of her disappearance on *Geraldo!*, and *Unsolved Mysteries*.

I was left alone in Mrs. Young's living room where she had set up an altar of personal information on Susan—with many of her personal items at my disposal. The items were as follows: a letter written in Susan's hand to her son, David; photos of Susan growing up; some research notes from her book with James Ridgeway of the *Village Voice*; her guitar, press portrait, and sunglasses.

During my "reading" I performed psychometry with the aid of a Key Quartz crystal as a "tool." Key Quartz, when used in psychometry, has the capability of picking up "information" in photos, items, etc., when it is laid upon them. The "information" is revealed via meditation and/or dreams.

I grew very attached to her sunglasses. No matter how many times I moved on to another item, her glasses summoned me back. I was met with "flashes" of Susan walking. She was wearing a short white skirt, white boots, and a white blouse. A black leather jacket covered this outfit. I "saw" her turn a corner and walk straight for a car. The car was dark in color. My first impressions were that it was a van or a limousine. Though there may be some discrepancy as to the vehicle, I am certain (and in agreement with sister-psychic Dorothy Allison, who spoke with Mrs. Young once prior to my becoming involved in the case) that Susan Walsh left of her own volition.

I am going to try to answer some of the questions asked me by Mrs. Young, in an attempt to hopefully shed some light on her daughter's disappearance and offer her some personal closure.

On September 18, 1997, I took the Key Quartz crystal and slept with it under my pillow. The following conclusions stem from my psychic impressions and from a dream.

The Dream/Vision

September 19, 1997, early morning hours, I awoke with a start. My breathing was belabored… ragged…heavy…and I felt I could not breathe. My heart was pounding fast and furious, and it was difficult for me to calm down. I sat up in bed and slipped the Key Quartz from under my pillow and held it in my hands, my eyes closed, all the while trying to take in slow, deep breaths. The dream unfolded before my eyes. In the dream, I was Susan on the inside, and she appeared as she did in life on the outside. She/I was running from someone who appeared to be Elvis Presley. He chased her/me through a brownstone apartment building. The inside of the building was pure white…the walls, the floors…doors…all white. No matter how fast she/I ran to get to each floor, he was one step ahead in the dream.

At one point, desperate and out of breath, she/I managed to get to a room moments before he did, but he was on the other side of the door...waiting. Susan/I was out of breath and heaving heavily, with a fast-beating heart as a result of the chase. I woke up.

My interpretation of this dream is as follows: the white represents spirituality and hospital care; the celebrity (Elvis) who did the chasing is someone of great power and wealth that wanted to get to Susan. The breathing was, of course, Susan's asthma and emphysema.

In conclusion, I believe Susan Walsh is alive and that she left of her own volition. Martha Young has said that Susan would never leave her young son, David, and can't understand why she would leave the house with not even her keys or anything, just her leather jacket....and say she would be back soon. My understanding is that Susan had no intention of returning. She had gotten herself into some uncomfortable situations with any number of people, and it is my belief that she feared for her life...from someone so powerful that the only way she could keep her family safe would be to go "underground" and lose her identity. She left her son David in order to keep him safe.

It is my estimation that Susan Walsh made her way across the US and eventually went to Florida, staying in the South Beach area. Things became too hot, and her emphysema had taken its toll on her health. I believe the "white" in my dream/vision is a hospital/convent run by Catholic nuns. Susan has taken a new name and cut her hair very, very short. She is very thin and ill. She is being tended to in this hospital and can stay as long as she wishes.

In closing, I would like to convey to Martha Young that she and her family are in my prayers. I hope I have provided helpful information. I believe God has led me to these conclusions. I can only wish that my participation sheds some light on her disappearance.

The Missing Florida Woman

One of the last missing persons cases I worked on via a law enforcement connection came through a client. Again, it was a desperate situation that led them in my direction. The trail for a missing woman in Florida had gotten cold, and they contacted my friend with the attitude that "you never know," in terms of what information I might pick up.

The information supplied to me was in an eight-by-ten manila envelope and was slipped under the door of my office while I was in session with a client. I got up the moment I saw it, and when I opened the door, there was no one in the outer office, and neither my client nor myself heard the outer door open or close.

Readings ended about six that evening, and before going home, I sat down and opened the envelope, dumping the contents onto my desk. There was a photocopy of her signature on a bank document, a snapshot of her alone and another with her two children and her husband. They were a nice-looking young family. She was in her thirties and very beautiful. They had been living in South America and had relocated to Florida when work was offered to the husband. Though he spoke English well, his wife didn't and was known to be withdrawn and kept to herself for fear she would be misunderstood.

Accompanying this was a letter from the family telling me what led to her disappearance. There was apparently a difference of opinion regarding what happened to her. The authorities believed her to be a thief who had stolen money, and her husband believed otherwise.

On the day her husband reported her missing, he had sent her to the bank, where she had withdrawn the family savings that amounted to about two thousand dollars. That was the last anyone saw of her. I put the papers down on the desk and leaned back in my chair and stared at her picture. I have always gone by my gut reaction, that first instinct—not the reaction that is impulsive but instinctual. There is a very fine line between them, and being impulsive in a missing person's case could result in dire consequences for the victim, the family, and/or law enforcement on the case. Erring on the side of caution and instinct was the only way to go.

I took a deep breath and frowned at her photo. This woman was not alive, and the more I looked at her, the longer that time frame became. I picked up the phone and called the client who had opened this all up to me.

"I don't get a good feeling about her."

"Do you know where she is? Or why she left with the money? It was money to pay insurance and taxes."

I sighed. "All I can say is that I believe she is still in the house."

"They have searched the house. Nada."

"I'm sorry I wasn't of more help. I'll keep them in my prayers."

There was a long silence on my client's end. "You don't think she's alive, do you?" It was more a statement than a question.

"No. And I don't believe she left the house once she returned from the bank."

After that conversation, I had not heard anything more about the case until I received another manila envelope slipped under my door with a note from my client. In it was an item clipped from a Florida newspaper local to her. I scanned the article. The missing woman had gone to the bank and withdrew cash, rather than a cashier's check. As she was walking out of the door, she met up with an assistant who worked in the town hall tax office. That part-time assistant was in a teasing mood and also a little prejudiced. He told her that she was late paying and would be thrown in jail. He said he hadn't thought anything of it. It was a joke, after all. But she did not understand it because she had all that money in her purse and now he was saying she was late and that there was nothing she could do about it. He went as far as to say she would lose her home.

She was scared. She hid with the money. She was found hanging from a noose in a closet in the attic with her purse and the two thousand dollars inside. The only reason she had been found was because a smell started to permeate the house after a time and she was discovered as the source.

I prayed for this woman, and I prayed for the bully who teased her to her death. Just because someone does not speak the same language does not mean they are incapable of communication. In most cases, they are usually far more eloquent and wise.

Chapter Twenty-One

HERE'S HOPING THE STARS GO WITH YOU

······································

WITH THE NEW office and the fresh start, I was excited to continue to practice the work I was coming to love. It didn't feel like work. It felt like I was connecting, and the network of connections kept growing with each experience. I was helping and making a difference for myself, too. I was also meeting some extremely fascinating people who one would normally refer to as a "character" when, in reality, they are just very gifted in their particular brand of insight. I have long learned that just because we don't understand something does not mean it isn't so. It also doesn't mean we are different; it means we are gifted, special, uniquely predisposed to something others may not have discovered or embraced yet. It most likely is an indication of what we lack in our knowledge of the particular subject at hand. I am open-minded and fair in my assessment of the things I experience because I believe those experiences are indeed the best teachers, if only we follow through with them.

So it was that I met a very unique individual in Pedro (not his real name), a fellow seer I met via the reading rooms on America Online (AOL). Back in 1995–1996, I had passed the requirements to do readings in their Crystal Ball Reading Room online, and Pedro was also doing readings, though not through AOL. We were both single, and our mutual interests kept us on the phone all hours of the night sharing the paranormal stories that happened to us, the music we liked to meditate to, and even the crystals we worked with.

During the summer of 1997, our e-mail and telephone communication continued for a few months, and then we met in person. This was not about romantic attraction but about psychic attraction and the desire to share with like-minded people. He had told me that he was not far from the Wanaque, New Jersey Vortex and was responsible for a lot of the paranormal discoveries that transpired there. I had heard enough stories from him and others about it to want to see the video and photographic evidence he had accumulated. But our initial in-person meeting was on my familiar territory, and I invited him to come to my new office.

"*And The Stars Go With You,*" he said, handing me a gift-wrapped box when I opened the door to my office suite.

"And also with you," I stammered in typical Catholic schoolgirl response. (Some habits die-hard!)

"No," he smiled and shook his head. "*And The Stars Go With You* is a meditation CD by John Serrie. You may have heard of it."

I laughed at my snafu and invited him inside the inner sanctum of my office space and to the reading room table.

"Have a seat." I motioned toward a chair. "Thank you, it's kind of you to give me a gift."

He blushed. "It's bootlegged."

"It's the thought that counts, and this was thoughtful." I put the box on the table and popped the tape into my player and sat down across from him. "Very trippy music!"

"There's more." He dug into his pocket, and as he did I took in his appearance. His hair was a light color, sort of like a mixture of brown and blond, and was tied back in a ponytail that trailed just past his shoulders. His eyes were blue, and he had a small goatee and a mustache. He wore a pair of black jeans with a conch belt and a blue denim shirt and comfortably worn-out leather boots. All this had been topped off with a cowboy-looking hat that he took off when he first arrived. He kept digging in the pocket of his jacket and finally pulled out a perfectly round "crystal" ball made of amber.

"Amber brings creativity and helps you follow your dreams while you accept the change around you. It will turn negative energy into positive. Keep it around when you work."

I took the amber ball into my left hand and gave it a gentle squeeze. It was warm, and it felt calming. It was light, almost weightless. "Thank you so much, Pedro."

"It will serve you well, I know it." He leaned back in the chair. "The moment I saw you pull up in your car next to mine in the parking lot, I could not believe how big your aura is," he said in admiration.

"Thank you…I think."

"Seriously. Your entire car was filled with this huge white bubble. You are a person who is pure of heart."

Now it was my turn to blush. I offered him tea, which I made from the water cooler I had in the room, and he asked if I could give him a reading. I did, and he took notes, nodding and pleased by whatever I was saying. When the reading was over, we chatted on the subject of angels, aliens, and UFOs. Pedro considered himself an expert in UFOs and aliens. I am a very skeptical person, and I have to be if I am to be an example to others, and when he said he had "evidence" and "proof," I wanted to see it.

"I owe you a reading," my fellow seer said. He wrote down his address on a slip of paper and pushed it toward me on the table. "I want to thank you properly, and I will give you a reading as well as go through some of the videos I have when you visit."

"Is that like going to see your etchings?"

He laughed. "Good one. If you want, please feel free to bring a friend."

In 1997 my frame of reference was completely changing. Because of my association with Pedro, I was now privy to things I had literally only read about. UFOs? Aliens? Considering what I was doing for a living, I was in no position to judge, however, I knew that it was important to explore anything that came my way. It might even prove to be beneficial to others who might be following my example.

It was in July and August when I first started visiting the white nondescript house that was camouflaged and hidden from the road by hedges all around it. I arrived alone, and Pedro led me downstairs to the finished, paneled basement that contained his video and computer equipment. I stared at the rows of monitors, each one with a different video on the screen. I came up to one, and Pedro pulled out a chair for me to sit down beside him.

"So this is Command Central?" My eyes riveted to a bulletin board that covered most of the wall and around the desk, and they scanned the photos and media he had pinned up there. "You don't miss much," I commented, my eyes returning to the screen in front of us.

"I try not to." He started to fiddle with the lights on the instrument panel in front of him. "I'm going to pull up some videos for you to look at." He clicked a few keys and turned a couple of knobs, and on came the first video.

To say I was amazed by what he presented would be a real understatement. The images were what I'd seen on television before, but never this close, and each video was shot at around the same time in the afternoon every day. He said they were "saucers and spaceships" and described them as they moved slowly through the sky, open only to the camera eye. There were high hats, cigar shapes, and orb-like vehicles speeding through the sky, normally undetected by the naked eye.

"This is for real?" I knew it was a rhetorical question, but the footage on the monitors was nothing short of amazing.

"Yes. Want to shoot one yourself?" He didn't wait for my answer as he picked up his camera and tripod and gestured for me to follow him back up and out of the house.

I watched him set up the tripod and snap the camera on top. "I'll shoot one, and you can shoot one." He started to peer through the viewfinder, when I stopped him.

"How will I know what I'm shooting at if I can't see it?"

He took his eye from the camera and looked at me. "You'll feel it."

I rolled my eyes. I had hated tests when I was in school, and nothing changed about that now as an adult, and I felt like this was a test of the psychic nature. "Are you testing me?"

Pedro shook his head. "No," he said simply. "Just like you, it helps me to have validation that what I'm seeing, in this case what is being filmed, is really happening. I trust you enough to feel your vibe understands that and can help confirm." He grinned. "Are you in?"

He waited for me to answer, and it felt like we stood facing each other for the longest time. Finally, I nodded. "I'm in."

The sky was clear and blue with very few clouds. Pedro pointed the lens up to the sky and began shooting, all the while shifting it ever so slightly to the right or left. After about ten minutes, he invited me to step in and film the skies on my own.

I lifted the lever and focused the camera upward, my eye scanning the vastness above us. A few fluffy clouds, a bird, and that was it. For the most part, the sky was void of anything remotely different than what I would expect. A short time later, we took the footage into the house to review. Lo and behold, there was that cigar-shaped image again! Pedro slowed down the footage, and we could then see an actual saucer-like image next to the cigar!

"Look at the time on the clock. That's your footage, Linda."

"I didn't see any of that," I explained in awe.

We looked at his recording, and he had two cigar shapes. I truly didn't know what to make of this, and I was open to this exploration so much that I visited there on a regular basis as he amassed a huge collection of unexplained footage.

After that first time when I took those videos with Pedro, I returned home electrified by the events and felt the world was filled with infinite possibilities, just like Deepak Chopra, Wayne Dyer, Marianne Williamson, and so many others have said. I fell asleep thinking about what I had encountered, the warm breeze from my open window lulling me into a relaxing sleep.

Buzzzzzzzzz...

The sound was soft and subtle, like an annoying little fly buzzing around. I turned my head and lazily looked over at the clock: 3:00 a.m. As the buzzing grew louder, my attention was drawn to the window across from my bed. It was too far away to reach without walking to, but not too far that I couldn't see what was on the other side of it. And there was definitely something there…a shape…

I tried to get up to look out of the window, but my body felt as if the bed was holding me down. I knew I wasn't paralyzed, but I couldn't move anything except my eyes, and the buzzing was getting even louder. I once again looked to the window. I squinted at the object taking shape as its sound became muffled again, the only light coming from the street lamp from the yard behind mine. I took a deep breath and let myself feel the energy around me. The object was silver-gray and had three lights across the front. It was making no sound now, and I remained perfectly still as this saucer-shaped object hovered quietly just outside my window.

Zap! Zap! Zap!

I felt a ray of energy aim straight for my third eye three times, and the object quickly disappeared from my window.

The next morning, I was personally charged, literally. Everything I touched gave me a shock! It took me an hour to blow-dry my hair, to no avail, because I came out looking like Don King; that is how highly charged my entire body was. I described this to my mother, my dream interpreter, because I was not sure if this was a dream or a visitation of some kind.

"Considering you look like lightning struck you in your sleep, I can't tell you to ignore it. My advice would be to be open to it as another way to understand energy." This wasn't exactly the kind of advice I wanted to hear, and she knew it. "Lin, I don't have all the answers." She gave me a kiss on the forehead. "Maybe you should think about taking a break from Pedro for a while."

"I enjoy his friendship."

"Then be phone or Internet friends. Keep the personal visits to a minimum. Don't let anyone take you off your own course, Linda. People mean well, but you have to remember to never give of yourself so totally to one person that you lose your own individuality."

"I like that. Can you write that one down for me?"

She laughed. "I'm paraphrasing yesterday's newspaper column by Ben Burroughs. I'll cut it out for you."

"You live by his quotes!"

"No, I'm empathetic to his sentiments."

From that point on, I began to experiment with how I sensed things in life. My perception of energy became all encompassing, as I could see, hear, touch, taste, and sense in a way that was making me very compassionate. My capacity to work with energy increased, and so intense was my sensitivity that I found that everything I touched had vibration to it. Intense and thick—like little shock waves. It is like that for me to this day. It's the reason for any bad hair days I have!

Pedro and I lost touch after a while, though we are both aware that we exist in the universal space of things. But he went his way, and I went mine, and because I did, I was able to put him in that sacred category of the teachers who have exchanged wisdom with me.

Chapter Twenty-Two

BARNES & NOBLE, OF COURSE!

....

"WE'D LOVE TO do an interview about you for our Entertainment section." The journalist introduced herself as representing *The Star Ledger,* our New Jersey newspaper.

That would be great as free advertising for my services in my home state, and I was grateful for the call because it would allow me to extend my reach. After spending a busy day in readings, it was a delightful call to receive.

"We heard you have been doing lectures and seminars at The Learning Annex in New York City and at some Barnes & Nobles bookstores to large crowds, and we wanted to send a photographer and journalist to interview you before the next one."

The timing was perfect, as my next Barnes & Noble appearance was a big one that was coming in the next month, March. My parents were really proud, and they came to my events in support, both of them loving to tell stories about me as a child.

Just as I was gaining momentum with an ever-expanding practice, our family was hit with two emergency situations, and both my mother and father were dealing with health issues at the same time. Life became even more demanding as I split my time between home care nursing, hospitals, and Mom's treatments. It took a huge chunk out of my days, but I was only too happy to help. I became her primary caregiver, which meant that I was responsible for driving her everywhere, because she had no license and therefore didn't drive. Many times I helped the radiation patients and their loved ones by sending Reiki healing energy to them, or helping them to learn some meditative deep breaths. The doctors started to look forward to my mother's treatments because my presence was making everyone feel better.

I also cooked her food, helped to wash and dress her when she eventually couldn't do it herself, made her appointments to see to her doctors, made nurse's calls, gave medication, and did anything else she might require. After awhile, I found myself tucking my parents in at night as they each lay side by side in bed in healing mode! I worked for their needs via an intercom. Sometimes one of them would inadvertently sit on the intercom, and the button would get stuck, and I would be hearing their entire conversations at three in the morning. I would trudge up the stairs and tell whomever it was that they were sitting on the button, then go back down the flights of stairs to bed.

For about fifteen months, we were hearing "she has six months," or "she has less than a year", or some such timeline that was decided a long time ago by a gaggle of doctors looking to get their names in prominent medical books. The power of positive thinking has no chance to help us with such negative motivation. The truth is that regardless of the illness, the time each of us has on this earth is different for everyone, and how that time affects us is different as well. It is easy to see how the transition of death can be hastened by the simple negative enforcement of words with a time line. If you tell a terminally ill patient that they have six months to live, then six months is all they will have, because you have already put into their minds that there is no reason to focus on healing. I didn't do that with my mother, and I immediately took her away from the one insensitive doctor who did.

Mom passed away on October 14, 1999, and autumn was our favorite time of year, but this year was different. The time of year had brought her downstairs to a hospital bed in the living room, and it was precipitated by nasty Hurricane Floyd, which turned out to be a catalyst for something far more life changing. A blackout had occurred, and I was literally flooded out of the basement apartment I was living in during her illness. I had just done a lecture at Barnes & Noble the week before to a packed house, and I was trying to take care of Mom and Pop (who had had heart bypass surgery) and work to pay the rent on my new Northfield Avenue office, all at the same time. Oh…and for my birthday I had just received the gift of a Jack Russell terrier puppy (I named Ginger) from a friend and client, and she was a handful!

I remember that weekend vividly. I had woken up to several inches of water and thought the dog had peed! But she was in bed beside me. I had gone up and down all day running errands, preparing meals, measuring meds, taking diabetic checks and then had hoped to go to bed earlier that evening, but Mom was on a backup generator, and everything was spoiling in the refrigerator.

That's where Susan Dolinko came in. She was a client who had become a good friend. She owned and operated a wine and liquor store in our town, and she is a very strong woman physically. If Mom fell out of bed and no one was there to help me, I would phone Sue. Bless her, she would close her store for the brief time and drive over to pick Mom up, make her laugh, and then go back to reopen. This particular weekend of the hurricane, she came to the rescue with two ice chests: one was filled with food, and the other contained cold drinks, like water, milk, etc. A third case was a duffel bag with flashlights, batteries, First Aid kit, and anything we needed to survive until power might be restored.

That Sunday night, I went down to the basement with some friends to survey the damage.

"Oh, man, this is bad." We looked around at what used to be the living room/bedroom area. The carpet was completely saturated and peeling already. The water was still high, rising high enough to ruin my bedroom furniture and any of the boxes that contained all my belongings. "I guess we start bailing."

We grabbed mops, brooms, and anything we could find to "sweep" the water level down so that we could peel up the carpet. In the process, we most likely swept up the gold and diamond cross Mom had given me for my twenty-first birthday.

My friends were pretty adamant that I could not possibly stay here, and the upstairs bedrooms were not doable for other reasons.

"You have to sleep somewhere. You can come home with us," my friend was saying. "You can't sleep here, Linda. You can't help your parents if you are in no condition yourself!"

He and his wife are lovely people, and I was grateful for the option, but they lived far enough away from my parents and my office that it would be stressful to add that commute into my days.

"Okay…okay…I know of one person who lives nearby who might have room." I picked up the phone and called Sue.

"You can stay here, but come now, because I have to get up early, and it's one in the morning!"

Fortunately, Sue had an entire suite (master bath, bedroom/sitting room, and an empty office) on the second floor of her home. She told me to stay as long as I wanted, and just before Mom died, I added the stress of moving what was left of my belongings to Sue's house about four miles away. That was September 18, and Mom passed away less than a month later. I was exhausted and in pain; even my teeth hurt. I was there with my mother, holding her in my arms as she drew her last breath. I am glad I was there for her last words, for in my time with my mother, there wasn't an "I love you" unsaid, and I am grateful for that.

Mom had been my champion and my cheering section. She was also my best friend. Doing my psychic work without her guidance was tougher than I thought it would be, but from the moment she left us physically, she was letting me know she was still there. I was picking up signs of all kinds that indicated she was trying to communicate with me, and I soon discovered that signs are very easy to miss if you don't make yourself aware of them. It's also easy to dismiss those you may be receiving because you want to receive them so desperately, and I'm no different than my clients. I want it etched in stone, too! That isn't always the case, but if you keep track of all the signs by writing them down in one book, the messages will be revealed over time. Looking back at that journal now, I am grateful for, and amazed by, the volume of the messages from Mom that accumulated.

The first sign came immediately after I left her house on the day she died. I had been making telephone calls for the funeral arrangements, to the point where my voice was hoarse. I stopped at a CVS store on my way home to buy a box of cough drops. Having been there before, I went directly to the aisle where I knew they would be.

CVS had every flavor except the one I wanted, which was cherry. I was checking to see if a couple of bags might be misplaced on one of the lower shelves, when I heard a loud smacking sound as something hit my leg. It was as if someone threw something at me from across the aisle. I reached down to what lay at my feet and picked it up, a smile spread wide on my face as the tears sprang to my eyes. I was holding a bag of CVS cherry cough drops, and there is no doubt in my mind that Mom is responsible for "tossing" it my way. A simple sign, but a powerful one when you consider that even as she made her transition she was still watching out for me.

As the funeral week moved forward, more signs represented themselves, and they weren't just for me, but friends and clients who knew Mom were calling with stories of their own. And now that I think about it, it seemed as if Mom was singling out certain people she knew would appreciate her humor and probably take the message back to me, which is exactly what happened.

"Linda, I'm so sorry to wake you, but your mother was just here, and now I can't get back to sleep!"

I sat up in bed and cradled the phone receiver under my chin. I recognized the whispering voice of my friend Randi. "What time is it? Is everything all right?"

"Yes...just...weird."

"Define 'weird,'" I asked as the fog cleared from my head. Randi was known for making a short story longer, and I figured this was going to take a while. She didn't disappoint.

"Okay...Can you hear me? Because I am in the walk-in closet so I don't wake the kids. They had a sleepover here last night and it's been crazy—"

"Randi!"

"Sorry...Okay, well, you know that the walk-in closet was just finished, right?" She didn't wait for an answer. "I decided to take advantage of free time from work and arrange my shoes in the new closet."

"All sounds very normal to me." I leaned back into my pillows.

"You'd think. Anyway, you know I have tons of designer shoes. It took me *hours*," she whined. "I put the kids to bed, took a bath with my new bath beads, and went to sleep." She blew out a long breath before continuing. When she spoke again, there was a slight tremor in her voice. "About a half hour later, just as I was dozing off, I heard a loud noise. I went to locate the sound and was led to the closet." She paused.

"*And*? Don't stop there!" I started to laugh just from the nervous tension.

"All of my neatly lined-up shoes were thrown around the closet! I had about a hundred pair of shoes in boxes all neatly labeled with a snapshot of the item taped to the outside of the box for easy reference. All of them were open! All of them were thrown around the entire closet as if someone ransacked it! Why, Linda? Why?"

I thought about this for a moment. "What makes you think that my mother is responsible?"

"Because she used to tease me about how much money I spent on shoes, and your mother *loved* shoes!"

"It's three o'clock in the morning."

"I know. I'm sorry." She was whispering again. "She's probably mad at me for something. What could she be mad about?"

"I have no idea. I'll talk to you tomorrow."

This was the first of several calls I received during that final week of good-byes. Some, like Randi's, were not exactly well received, but her last visits to other people would prove to be downright funny, and the right people received those messages. One of them was my Uncle Joey. They used to have a running joke, and she would refer to him as "you, devil you!" because of some of his teasing. He was the next call I received the following morning. His voice was deep and raspy, and he was laughing really hard as he relayed his own paranormal experience.

"You know how I pride myself in looking my best, Linda," he was saying.

"Yes, I do."

"I think Frances doesn't want me to wear my new shoes."

I laughed. "Why is that?"

"The morning after she died, I was searching for my new black shoes to wear for her wake and funeral. I've searched all the closets, but the only shoes I can find are my sneakers! I can't wear sneakers to my sister's funeral!"

That morning he did put the sneakers on so that he could buy a new pair of shoes. While he was walking around the house, he felt something sticking to the bottom of one. Looking down, he saw that there was a piece of paper there. He reached down and peeled it off. When he brought it up to see what it was, he found it to be a small piece of an envelope with the numbers 666 on it, the biblical sign for the devil.

"Your mother always teased me and called me 'the devil,' and I think she's saying that now."

This being the second shoe story I had heard since her passing, I guess you could say, apparently, Mom had a foot fetish when she first passed. I had my own experiences to add to the list. On the night she died, the alarms in the house went off for no reason, loud sounds were heard in the house, and I was having visions of her in all the mirrors, over and over again. Then poof! She'd be gone!

I was receiving all the "signs" that felt like Mom was spiritually with me. However, I could also apply reason to many of them, explaining them away and ultimately convincing myself that I hadn't received a valid sign after all. What I needed was what I often gave to my clients and friends: proof beyond a shadow of a doubt that a message was sent to me by my mother from the afterlife. That was what I was waiting and praying for. Until then, I kept my reading schedule light and went about my days going through the stages of grief as best as I could. It helped that my father was still alive, because it helped to keep her memory alive, too.

Chapter Twenty-Three

THE DIVINING MOMENT—A SPIRITUAL VISIT

....

I PRESSED THE BUTTON for the little electric candle (whatever happened to real candles?), said a prayer, and walked slowly back down the center aisle of St. Joseph's church and out to my car in the parking lot. It had been three days since my mother was buried. I had promised her I would light a candle when that third day arrived, because she believed it would hasten her trip to heaven. I deferred to her wishes, even though my own life was not so seeped in superstition.

When she died, everything around me suddenly took on an intensely sentimental and emotional meaning. The clothes I wore, the house I lived in, the television shows I watched, even the car I drove suffocated me with sadness. Everything I once took for granted that had included her now became a source of memories that pulled at my heartstrings. And after this church visit, I had to head back to that same car alone, never to share a physical ride with her again, and I was desperate for the communication we once had.

My having a practice as a psychic consultant kept Mom motivated to help me in any way she could. She not only took responsibility for nurturing the "gift" she was convinced I was born with, but she made sure she was with me for the most important moments in my early career. She helped me set up my first office and booked my first psychic "party" for group readings. She fielded questions from my clients while entertaining them with stories of my childhood. She did everything to be a part of my psychic experience and in so doing was able to experience and develop a sharper intuitive awareness herself.

With thoughts of her filling my head, I stepped into my Mazda, shoved the key into the ignition, and leaned back against the headrest with a long, deep breath. What would I do now? How would I continue without her guidance? Wouldn't it be a blessing if she could still communicate with me? I felt powerless to answer these questions.

As a working psychic, a few times in my life I had experienced communication from those who have passed away. But I didn't think I could actually bring someone through from there. On top of this, my mother—my friend, guide, and teacher—was not convinced that many people who said they were mediums were real mediums. She didn't want me to fall into a negative category, which is what movies and books have done to the profession in terms of medium abilities. I don't think she fully understood it. Mom was of the opinion that communication with the dead only happened in dreams or by happenstance but never through deliberate invitation. Because of this, I made a point of steering away from addressing the other side when I did readings, choosing to focus on the living and their concerns about finance and romance. My mother's death changed all that. I desperately wanted her to communicate with me. Would her beliefs prevent her from doing so? If not, then how could I make it happen?

The cell phone in my purse started ringing and startled me back to awareness. I reached in for it and flipped it open, grateful for the interruption. It was my father. He had been sorting Mom's things and wanted me to lend a hand.

"I just came back from lighting a candle for her," I said. "I'm only a few blocks from the house. I can come over now and see what you have."

"It's mostly paperwork. Your mother saved everything," he answered, reflecting on their fifty years together. "But that was part of why I loved her."

"I know, Dad," I said patiently, having heard this same thing before. "I know."

As I often did when driving alone since her death, I talked to her. I held long, one-sided conversations about everything that was on my mind. And, almost always, when I was done, I felt a whole lot better. I wasn't sure if Mom could hear me, but I knew someone was listening, and that was what I needed.

I started to talk to her now. "I wish we had agreed on one specific sign before you died, Mom. It would have made things a whole lot easier." I thought a moment about how she had refused to face the fact that her particular case of cancer was inoperable and thus terminal, instead choosing to sustain herself on the faith that God would hear her prayers. Though it did sustain her far longer than most patients in her position, I just wish we had prepared more.

"Now, I have to find a way to communicate with you," I said aloud. "You may not have believed in inviting the abilities of mediums, but I know you believed in me and in signs, and I know you believed that those who died could come through on their own if they had good reason." I paused the car at the stop sign at the corner of my father's street. "Give me a sign, Mom. Show me that you can hear me."

My father gave me a big hug when he opened the door. "Come into the dining room, honey. I've got Mom's box in there."

My brother was painting, and the rooms were covered with drop cloths. Stepping over them, I gave my brother a smile and followed behind Dad. "Is this it?" I asked, positioning myself beside a substantial carton.

He nodded. "You want to stay for coffee?" I shook my head, and he picked up the box. "Then let me take this out for you."

We walked back out to the car, and he placed the box on the front seat next to me. "Be good." He reached in for a good-bye kiss on the cheek and walked slowly back to the house.

I looked over at the box, shook my head, and took a quick peek inside. Family recipes, old Christmas and birthday cards, and envelopes of photographs that never made it to her photo albums were the legacy she left. I felt an immediate sense of peace just having the box near me.

I took the long way home along some of the prettier back roads. Autumn was always my favorite time of year, and I remembered taking the same roads with Mom in the passenger seat. I started to talk to her again. This time, though, I was feeling so overwhelmed by the flood of memories coming from the box that I began to cry. The tears stung, and I couldn't see well, and I had to slam on the brakes, stopping just short of a red light. The box tumbled off the seat, and I watched transfixed as one single piece of paper slowly sailed out of the box like a feather and floated onto the car floor. I reached down and turned it over. It was a recipe written in Mom's handwriting. My fingers glided along her neatly written script across the page, and as they did, I felt tiny little electrical charges connect with my fingertips. The charges seemed to pulsate warmly throughout my body, and I was suddenly filled with the positive awareness that Mom was sitting right there in the car with me. The longer I held the recipe in my hand, the more intensely I felt this. My heart started to race furiously, and I could feel a hot flash insinuate its way over my body before it exploded in a burst of sweat. She was here! I wanted to scream the words, but I found I could not speak. I sat frozen and shaken as a wave of dizziness overcame me. The light turned green, and I clumsily pulled the car over to a side street and shoved it into park.

"Mom?" I leaned back against the seat, closed my eyes, and allowed myself time to calm down and resonate with her energy. With my next deep breath, I saw an image of her behind my closed lids, a picture in my mind's eye not unlike when she was alive and well.

As the picture faded, I felt a magnet-like force of energy return my attention to the recipe in my hand. I opened my eyes. I still felt light-headed, but the dizziness had subsided. "I can't believe your reason for contacting me was to make sure I passed on one of your recipes," I said out loud. I didn't expect to receive a reply, but I was new at this and didn't really know how it worked. I was psychically experienced enough, however, to know that my mother's spirit was in my car, and I had invited her in via the very piece of paper in my hands. It acted much like an invitation.

I sat up and took another deep breath. All this time I thought that being a medium involved having to actually see those who died. It never occurred to me that the very energy I read for my living clients is the same energy they will have when they die. Energy manifests into various forms that are not always seen. That is what I believe is happening when people on the other side "reveal" themselves to a medium. They are doing so through the manifestation of energy, and anyone who is in tune with energy will be able to experience the other side once they understand that and decipher messages.

So there I sat in the car on the side of the road, fully aware that my mother's energy sat beside me, a sense of peace finally lending itself to me as I reasoned this all out. She was here. But, why? I still didn't know what her message was. I looked down at the paper again in search of a clue. The recipe was for her traditional Italian Easter Meat Pie, and she only made it that one time a year without exception. I kept turning it over in my mind. Meat pie. Easter. Recipe. A voice in my head whispered those words over and over. I repeated them aloud. "Meat pie. Easter. Recipe. What are you trying to say...?"

And then it hit me, and the message became so clear that I could not believe I had almost missed it. It wasn't about the meat pie or the recipe itself. It was about Easter and what that time of year meant. Easter is about the crucifixion and resurrection of Jesus Christ. Easter Sunday is celebrated as the day Jesus rose from the dead to join His father in heaven. He was not really dead but had risen to a place with a higher vibration. Just as that was the message given to His mother and the apostles those many years ago, so was it the message I received from my own mother now. She had risen. She was at peace. And best of all, she was still here in energy, and I needed only to call upon that energy to communicate with her.

The very moment I acknowledged this as the message, I knew I was right, for I could feel her energy slowly pull back and away from me. Soon, it dissipated altogether, and I was once again alone. But now something was different. I had invited someone from the other side, and she had accepted my invitation. I was now a willing communicator with this energy.

Chapter Twenty-Four

SEDONA, ARIZONA, AND THE RED ROCKS

·····································

AFTER MY MOM passed away, Sue talked me into taking a trip to Sedona, Arizona, for some relaxation from the grief I was feeling. It was a great suggestion, but I kept thinking it wasn't going to happen. So I really didn't do much to create the awareness for the trip. I have to credit Sue for rectifying that. She forced me to get new luggage and helped me pick out a wardrobe for the trip.

I don't remember much about the flight except I was by the window seat. Maybe I wanted to be closer to the angels in case the inevitable happened. It was a pleasant flight, it didn't feel too long, and when we arrived, we were pretty elated.

So nowadays I wasn't checking into a hotel with my friend, Nina. I hadn't seen her in a while. I was checking into a kitchenette suite with two bedrooms with Sue, after having boarded our dogs, which I hate doing because I love traveling with my dog.

We rented a Mustang convertible and headed for the Sedona Hilton, with Sue driving and the top down. It was oppressively hot, and that top did not stay down for long before we closed the rental up tight and turned on the AC. The moment we hit town, we noticed a shift in the energy. I felt light-headed, and I was trembling from the high vibrations of the area. We had both read a great deal about the spiritual vortexes in Sedona, and many people had visited to meditate with their energy. We looked forward to experiencing that ourselves.

The suite had a beautiful balcony that overlooked the great red rocks, and the beauty of the place enthralled me. What I didn't care for was the commercialism, which was rampant by then. I wished I could have experienced Sedona pre-tourist trap, when it was more about the force and the people than it was about selling anything to a tourist if they believed the story you told them. This was the first time I was exposed to a side of the alternative lifestyle that many people described as "a New Age mecca," a name that labeled a craze and made me feel very uncomfortable with the mixed messages provided. All this was further confirmed by the rows of shops and high-priced items designed to lure in people looking for spiritual and metaphysical help.

Not to be deterred, we continued with our plans during that week and enjoyed some very powerful meditations on the various vortex areas. We usually planned them for when we would least likely run into tourists. Not that we weren't tourists in our own right, but our purpose and intention to meditate was different than what normally attracted people there.

While walking the path around Bell Rock for a morning meditation, I caught sight of something that looked like it had a face in it. I am fully aware that people can see faces and such in objects like rocks and trees, etc. (In fact, it's referred to today as "matrixing.") But I didn't feel like I was seeing something that was not deliberately put there for me to see. I felt it was a sign and an answer to my prayers. I kneeled down, and upon closer examination I could see the shape of a man's head and torso...and halo? Some sort of light was around him, and he looked as if he was holding a staff. I saw the image of Jesus, and I referred to it as the Jesus Stone. It never occurred to me to that it wasn't right to take the rock, but we did, and Sue lugged it back up to the car in 105-degree heat!

Whenever I travel I set up a sacred space in the bedroom. I usually have a cloth, a bell, perhaps an angel or religious icon, and a candle. I add flowers later and often take along a special crystal. I placed the Jesus Stone on my little altar, did my nightly meditation, and went to sleep, and that's when the crazy dreams started. I heard a female voice say to me: "The elders have blessed you with a snapshot of faith. Return the rock to its home in gratitude for the blessing."

It took me a few moments to realize that I was not dreaming, and I was compelled to pick up my Canon and shoot a couple of photos of the rock. When I went back to bed, I slept soundly. I told Sue about it the next day over breakfast.

"Oh my God, please don't tell me I have to carry that rock all the way back on that trail!"

"I'll help," I promised.

"How are you going to help? Are you going to be a lookout or something? For God's sake, Linda, this sucker is heavy."

"Yes, Sue, that is exactly why we are doing it…for God's sake."

She shook her head. "Give me the damn rock." And we were off to return it. The heat that day was about 106 in the shade!

The last thing I remember hearing is Sue walking in front of me on the hot trail, mumbling to herself, "First she's got me carrying crystals at the beach in a borrowed bowling cart, and now this!"

I could not stop laughing.

The Ruins

The next to last day, we took a tour with a guide and a group of people to visit ancient Native American historic sites. As we walked around the mountainous terrain of layered rock, I began to feel off-kilter and extremely dizzy. When the guide stopped for us to rest, I leaned against one of the huge layered rocks to catch my breath. As we hiked around and up the trail, I fully realized that the altitude was different than I was used to and could make me dizzy; however, this was even more intense than it should have been.

"You okay?" I wasn't sure, but I nodded and stayed where I was for a few more moments. The guide instructed me to take some of my water and then turned to address the group. "The energy here is very old and can, coupled with the altitude, make you disoriented. Drink plenty of water."

Sue and I stood leaning against the rock as the others climbed around the area in exploration. She asked if I was okay, and when I opened my mouth to answer, nothing came out. Instead, I tilted my head, mouth open, and pitched my ear forward to hear better.

"What's going on?" Sue asked.

When I looked at her, it was as if she were a million miles away from me, and the further away, the more my ear picked up a sound that I thought was of children crying. The crying grew louder, and I felt dizzier, finally bending over at the waist and sobbing into my hands. Sue didn't know what to do, and I didn't know what was happening to me, but I was becoming very sick. My body went down in temperature, and my teeth were chattering even though it was 103 degrees, then suddenly I felt like it was so hot my pressure would explode. All around me I felt grief and sadness; the energy of hurting children was everywhere. Gripped by the power of their pain, my hands flew to my solar plexus (waist), and I began to do Reiki healing on myself.

The tour guide made quick steps over to me, and soon the rest of our companions on this journey had gathered around and joined us.

"Is she okay? What's going on? What happened?"

I could hear the questions, but my concentration was on clearing my head enough to stand upright.

"The children." I said. "They are everywhere."

"What about the children?" Our guide escorted us over to a circle of rocks where we could sit down, and the action was enough to, gratefully, break the negative connection I was having.

"What children?" someone else asked.

Our guide put up his hand and shook his head to halt further questions. "Not everyone hears the children." He looked at me. "What do you do for a living?" he asked suddenly.

"Linda is a psychic medium," Sue clarified.

"I got very dizzy and felt sick. At the same time I could hear children crying and felt an overwhelming sadness that made me feel physical pain. I don't know what happened."

As our group of ten listened, he told us more about the spot where I had been standing, as well as the layers of steps that led up the mountain. They weren't really "steps" at all. They were graves. The site was one huge burial ground.

"The people were poor." He picked up a stick and cleared away some of the dirt in front of us. "Medical help was not open to them. Many people died, and most were children. If a child died, they were buried underneath the front doorway, where you were standing. These ruins are very old, and many of these burials go down into the earth and rise for over twelve stories."

That elicited a collective gasp, and I wasn't the only one who was feeling literally sick at the thought of being right on top of so many graves. But now it was making sense for me. I leaned forward in fascination as he continued.

"Homes were built on top of each other into the side of the mountain. The energy that made you sick are the energies of the dead who are buried at each entrance, on each of the twelve stories of homes in this mountain."

My fellow travelers became quite animated at that point, and they considered the tour a great success. Personally speaking, I took away something very different from this visit. I discovered that my ability for empathy could be dangerous. As much as I enjoyed the work I was doing, there was cause for me to protect myself from the emotions of others. I vowed to work on a meditation CD as soon as I got home that might help others clear their energy fields so they might not be so empathetic to sadness or negativity.

Chapter Twenty-Five

ONE DOOR CLOSES, ANOTHER OPENS—LETTING SPIRIT MOVE ME

···

I WAS STILL WORKING out of the same offices where the angels had helped us when Mom and I were locked in the building during that strange weekend. The difference with then and now was not just the dawn of a new millennium, but I was entering it grieving and without my mother's intuitive guidance. It was a very insecure feeling, and I needed to be grounded in something to take my mind off of my overwhelming emotions.

Over the course of this time, Sue expressed an interest in becoming a part of my business. We talked about goals and played around with ideas and thoughts as to what that business might be like. We already knew it had to be an extension of my work and belief system, but we also knew that presentation was everything if we wanted to reach, and help, people to understand that. Call me crazy, but I actually thought this was a good idea, and we began thinking of names for the company.

We settled on Embracing The Universe, fondly trading as ETU, which you can take further to mean "and you," in Italian. But I digress.

We got ourselves incorporated, and Sue, as VP and business manager, took on the appointment calendar and much of the administrative work. I was doing the readings and working much of the creative side via websites, blogs, and promotional writing. Up until this time, I had relied on the help of friends as my "assistants" and my mother as an advisor. This new business with Sue was exciting, and I looked forward to it.

The only problem was getting my following to not hang up the phone when we answered "Embracing The Universe," because they thought it was a wrong number! The solution to that was to add a codicil to incorporation and become Linda Lauren's Embracing The Universe. This was 2000, and branding was not what it is today. In our present world, branding has become the new goal. Everyone is a brand, and they are promoting them by not even moving from their desktops, offices, or even beds to advertise. Posting and tweeting is the personal PR foundation for getting the word out. Meanwhile, Skype, iChat and FaceTime are my new ways to meet and socialize "face-to-face." Not having those advantages did not put us at a disadvantage. Rather, it required us to be more creative to keep our following on a personal level.

Now that we had this new company, we felt we should expand to a different location. We found a nice suite in Livingston, a town over from my present office, and I reluctantly agreed to move. Besides, there were so many strange things happening when I worked at the old place at night that I had taken to having Sue's big dog, Peri, accompany me. If the client was "okay," then Peri would sit by the client. But if Peri found that person questionable, he would sit stoically by me. And we were both a little unnerved by some of the goings-on in the office space. The window by the desk closed *and* opened by itself during the readings of many of my clients. Not to mention the fact that on more than one occasion, Peri and I heard the outside door to the suite open and close while we were in the inner sanctum of the reading room. The sound was usually followed by footsteps and the shadow of feet walking past the door! Peri would bark, and I would hesitantly open the door to find no one there.

Perhaps I was not as reluctant to leave as I remember when I take into consideration some of the paranormal experiences that occurred in that space.

Chapter Twenty-Six

MAJOR DEVELOPMENTS

· ·

I BELIEVE IN THE existence of angels and guides and gain strength and comfort from them. One of my favorite abilities is to recognize the angels/guides I encounter when I am in a reading with someone. A session with me is always about communication, trust and awareness, and that is best defined and expressed behind closed doors in the safe haven of my Reading Room. I learned much of this through my own guides, especially one I soon encountered.

That winter brought with it a snowstorm, and we got together with some friends to play the game Upwords. I love board games, especially word games, and this one was a favorite of mine when Mom was alive. In fact, the very game we were using had actually belonged to her, and I knew this by her signature (literally) on the inside of the box! My mother was known to label everything, and even our games were not exempt from a nametag. (I can recall my adolescent friends marveling at my name because it was beautifully embroidered on the inside of my clothing, from collars to cuffs. Mom was very creative that way, and my friends could not believe that the tags were hand sewn. I can't imagine how long it took to embroider my entire maiden name: Linda Gialanella, but she did, and it was amazing!)

So we sat down in front of a roaring fire and played Upwords in hopes that the snow would abate by the time we were done. But the white, fluffy stuff kept falling, and everyone had left, but Sue and I, and we continued to play the game. I was keeping the score, and my hand was poised to write down her tally. I could feel my hand get heavier, as if someone had covered it and was forcefully, yet gently pushing it down to the pad to write. I didn't say anything to Sue as the blue ink touched the green-lined steno pad we were using.

As I began to dialogue with him through writing, I learned that Major is my personal spirit guide, and along with him came a group known as The Collective, angels and guides of others who would be there to help me deliver messages. Over the years, he has revealed tidbits of information that explores our relationship and who he was to me when he was alive. A specific time that covers my past life connection with Major is the period of 1862 to 1920, with special emphasis on The Civil War. This steno pad became one of the first of the many journals I now have compiled on our communication.

Remember that window I was drawn to at the Gettysburg Visitor Center back in 1994 that had a quartz crystal left in the pocket of the Confederate soldier? Well, that was no "accident" that I aimed straight for it to take that picture; he explained to me that he had been responsible for giving the crystal to the soldier. It originally belonged to him. Oh…and the soldier who seemed to "disappear" behind the tree that night by Gettysburg College campus?

That was him, and he did, indeed, go by the name "Major," the word I whispered without knowing why. Here was my answer. A guide was revealing himself to me, and I was excited for the future as he shared through my pen (and later through my keyboard) a way to automatically connect and communicate with a messenger of higher wisdom. Major had come to be with me so that we might work together to help to spiritually empower the people we would meet.

This is what I know about him through his communication and what I have had confirmed to me through intense research and documentation

He said he did not enlist, because he was too young, but he did "serve" and help the Union effort. In 1862, at the age of about nine, Major ran away to join the troops during the Civil War and was turned away for reasons unknown. That did not deter him as he traveled to each encampment and did various odd jobs for the war effort.

He was enlisted to help President Lincoln secure and transfer documents. His assistance in tracking and transporting those secret documents was invaluable to ending the war. He received a long letter from President Lincoln, who fondly referred to the adolescent as "Major," as a sign of respect for his bravery in coming to the aide of his country.

Major and The Collective are a blessing. I am grateful that my belief in God has allowed angels and divine spirit to guide and assist me as a result of my openness to infinite possibilities.

Chapter Twenty-Seven

GUARDIAN ANGELS—
FRIENDS IN HIGH PLACES

....

THERE ARE TWO photos of a house in the photo section of this book. You've probably seen a house very much like it in the movies or on television. The architecture suggests that it's haunted, its size and windows hinting that something dark and sinister might be going on inside. It is the perfect façade for a good horror movie. In truth, this is a house like many other older, stately homes in northern New Jersey and a sign of nineteenth-century affluence. What sets it apart from others is the frozen moment in time within which this and the other photograph were taken.

The house was not the intended subject as much as the previous tenant, whom I heard came from more genteel days. Friends who knew her said that the house once belonged to a spinster recluse who had died in a fire. The third floor of her house was where she was said to have spent most of her happy times, whether alone or when infrequently entertaining. So it was no surprise that the third floor appeared to be a hotbed of spirit activity. I sensed that the orbs in the photo of the third floor window and above the house were there as guardians for anyone who lived in her house since her death.

The other window on the third floor has a strand of orbs streaming from the window in tunnel fashion. I didn't sense this as having an identity. Rather, I took this to be a vortex of spiritual passage—an actual access portal through dimensions that was the way in which the energy in the photo manifested after it arrived.

As I looked to the night sky to snap this, I felt as though these divine visitors were gathering in welcome. I had no preconceived notions as to what this photo shoot would achieve, yet I had a vibrant sense of warmth that curled itself around my body like a gentle hug just before taking the picture.

Special Note:

It's important to keep in mind that not every white circle or orb in a photo is spirit. More often, the "orb" is actually dew or dust in the air or on the camera lens, or even a camera strap or thumb in the way. There is always the likelihood of environmental residue creating the array of orbs we photograph. The only way I "know" what I have captured is spirit is because I am a medium and recognized spirit within the orb. Again, I want to reinforce that I do not believe every orb is a manifestation of spirit. There are tests, conditions, and specific awareness of the paranormal to take into consideration before an orb is defined as spirit, but as a medium, for me it is instant.

Guardian Angel

My mother taught me a guardian angel prayer when I was a child. I had come home from playing at a friend's house and asked her what a guardian angel was and if I had one, too. Mom patiently painted a glowing picture for me of a white-winged being who loved and guarded me as one of God's children. She said the prayer was an invitation to my guardian angel to play with me. She told me that angels were "divine energy," and such energy was white, bright, and beautiful. This photograph has forever confirmed that childlike perception of my mother's description.

I invited my friends Sue and Todd for an evening of paranormal investigating with our camera equipment. We drove slowly by the opulent houses of the nearby neighborhood. I had thought I'd taken my last picture of the night, but as I was bending to get back into the car, I had one of those "second-thought" moments. Should I take another? Shouldn't I? I stepped back up to the curb, leaned against the car, and paused. Just a quick moment prior to pointing my camera, I whispered to my angels, guides, and family who had passed on (I wanted to cover all bases) to please send me a sign that they were there, watching over me. I clicked the shutter and got quickly back into the car.

Sue and Todd came over to my house the next day to review the results of our evening. I hooked the digital camera up to the television screen for easier group viewing, and we sat down on the couch in anticipation. Advancing the cartridge forward, I was literally skipping one, when Sue pointed and asked me what the white light was to the right of the TV screen. I zoomed in and brought the image to a tighter close-up and then magnified it again. Large or small, the shape did not change. The glowing light source appeared to have wings in movement and was hovering protectively. Upon even closer observation, there were no "eyes" and therefore unlikely to be a bug. Besides, it was not that type of an evening when the photo was taken. This image looked remarkably like what my mother had described an angel would look like, and it felt like it was light and vibrant, and I could especially tune into an energy that stemmed from the windows. It took me a moment to comprehend what we were actually looking at. I sat mesmerized with the rest of the group as a calmness and comfort draped over us that we could not explain.

Defying practical explanation, this photograph has increased my faith in all things paranormal. No matter who sees it, those who understand spirit cannot refute what it represents. It is a portrait of divine spirit energy. I am forever grateful for this angelic episode in my life that verifies for us the existence of consistent angelic guidance in photographic representation.

Chapter Twenty-Eight

INSPIRATION & VISION UNLEASHED

···

I F YOU CAN imagine what it would be like to uncork something that contains wonderful insight and creative vision, put it in a bottle, and have it explode all over your being with utter joy and inspiration, that would best describe what took place for me as the new millennium and new decade unfolded. There were so many ideas coming to me in dreams and as we brainstormed in our business meetings that I was literally moving from one project to the next with speed.

The Angel Logo

The first consideration was the logo of this new business endeavor we were creating. What would best represent us? We agreed on an angel, and I recruited an artist friend to come up with a drawing, but it didn't speak to me. And this angel really had to speak to me, as I wanted it to represent my connection spiritually. Public domain clip art and graphics were all over the Internet, but I wanted something personal that we created and owned.

One night, while I was sitting at the keyboard, playing with a few of the color and "paint" programs available, I sat with my hand on the mouse, looking at a blank page with a white background on the screen. The color I was going to use was blue, but I hadn't a clue what I was going to draw. My mother was a better artist than I am, and I had wished that she was there to guide my hand. I closed my eyes.

My hand felt heavy, again (just as with Major) as if someone was pressing down on it so that I would move the mouse. I didn't fight it, and soon the "touch" became lighter, and my hand began to move of it's own accord. I knew about automatic *writing* but this was *drawing*!

I opened my eyes and watched my hand move up and around the canvas of the computer screen in one, long squiggle stroke. At the end of the stroke, my hand moved to the top of the drawn image and encircled the top of it. My hand was released, and I rolled my chair back to see the results.

It was an angel! That one long stroke looked like an angel! And the circle on top was an obvious halo. We had our logo! She has gone through a change of color since then: she's lavender and is encircled in an orb, but she is the same amazing vision that embraced my personal universe that day.

The Hope Deck™

My late mother and I loved acronyms. We would play all kinds of word games, but acronyms were always a favorite. When I first came upon the idea of creating a deck of cards based on acronyms, I never expected to be a part of such a divine process. Though I believe that all things we create are with the help of a higher power, I had never experienced how subtle that message could be, and how intense the outcome. This deck is evidence of what can be done when you truly let go and let God and the universe provide.

While Mom was still alive, I had started to make a list of words that I felt were positive motivators to live by. Everyday words took on a spiritual and self-empowering meaning when the acronym was applied.

I spent the next several months productively driven at the keyboard of my computer, using it as therapy. Within two months, I had produced, written, and artistically designed a deck of twenty-six cards. Sue began to laminate them into three-by-five "cards," and we tested them on a few friends. I decided to call it The Hope Deck™ because embracing hope is our intention as well as our mission statement.

The reception our prototype deck received was life altering. People got it. And now we made the official deck available for sale to all of my clients! Each card in the deck is meant to act as your personal psychic, and it assists you in leading a more self-empowered life by meditating on the cards as you choose one regularly.

The feedback I got was along the lines of: Who wouldn't want to get a shot of positive reinforcement every day?

Graceful Meditations with Linda Lauren (CD)

It was only natural that the process continued, leading me to produce a meditation CD. My earlier attempt was, upon reflection, very humorous. It was a cassette tape with my voice guiding clients to breathe via the use of sound effects from a noise machine. You know the kind: waterfalls, babbling brooks, and ocean sounds. It was ingenious because it was a way to get my clients to meditate and to understand my teaching of meditation so that they could develop a routine. I was that desperate to get everyone to meditate! I wanted the world to embrace the joy, peace, and wisdom that I did when in mindfulness.

Someone once asked me: "Why should we meditate when we already pray?"

I have always felt that prayer was like asking a question and meditation was waiting for the answer. Why would you not want to meditate?

Graceful Meditations, as we fondly referred to it, was something I scripted to help people develop the healthy habit of meditating regularly. I kept three things in mind for the recording: teach people to breathe, guide them in the meditation, and make the meditations short enough to instill the desire to do it again. Too long and you could lose them; too short and it had no benefit. So, I settled on two ten-minute meditations, and my friend, Bob Vidal, scored the background music.

When used regularly, meditation helps you to manage day-to-day stress with soothing results, and even lower blood pressure.

Both of these products had me meditating even more, and I was enjoying picking one of my cards each day to help motivate my mood with positive energy. We had parties to introduce them and shared with our guests the new tools for self-empowerment. I was proud to be able to share the light that I embrace, and embracing this particular light helped me extend my reach in a way that helped others to feel better. That is what I wanted to do: make a difference by enlightening people into feeling better!

The Vibe™ Room Energy Spray

I have always used prayer and Native American sage as a means for clearing a space of negativity, however, I felt that there was something missing in the equation. It was great to be able to clear the room, but what about raising the vibration? I experimented with herbs and essential oils for over a decade and decided to create a recipe that combined specific essential oils, sea salt, a special family element, and even crystals. I tested combinations and kept a journal on how I felt when I used them. I had clients and friends test the products, and their subsequent journals proved invaluable to my research and development. I finally came up with something that not only did the job to make people feel wonderful, but it smelled wonderful, too!

COP (Charms Of Protection) ™

Yes, there is that penchant for acronyms again! I was on a roll in the creativity department, and I saw no sign of it abating and was eager for the next item on the Angel Agenda in my head. This was created for protecting the spirit and to help with issues. It is a variation of that pouch my Grandma Anna had made that Mom and I found after my uncle died.

By uniting crystals and charms chosen specifically for your own personal vibration, I created this powerful talisman. Each one is spiritually "charged" with prayer and Reiki healing energy. I made it for people to embrace peace, security, love, and healing. People often ask, "Where is a cop when you need one?" Look no further.

Chapter Twenty-Nine

ANGELIC ANSWERS—
GOOD-BYE, MAMA

....

W E CALLED MY mother's mother "Mama." She was a phenomenal dressmaker and seamstress and Mama preferred visiting psychics to being one. Many times over the years, I heard stories of Mama traveling to see Grandma in Newark for a "visit," which was most likely a session. The psychic nature of things was an interestingly positive aspect of their lives as in-laws.

Mama lived about twenty-seven years longer than Grandma, and we were naturally closer because of that. She also didn't live far (and was close to where I worked), and I visited her often. She lived alone with her poodle in a cute house, and for all her ninety-six years, she was far from feeble. However, her life began to end the day she fell in July 2001. She had been alone and had forgotten she wasn't the young and strong woman she used to be. The aide who came in the mornings found her on the floor of her den, after having a heart attack when she tried to move the television set. She had broken her hip and her pelvis. When I got the call, I rushed to the hospital. On the way out the door, I grabbed a small figurine of an angel in a blue dress and asked Sue to come with me for moral support.

Fifteen minutes later I was pushing through the doors of the ER, Sue right behind me, the angel figurine clutched in my hands. We found Mama lying in one of the beds against the far wall. She smiled when she saw us.

"I can't believe I did such a stupid thing," she said, wincing in pain with each word. "I fell, Linda."

"I know, Mama." I reached over and took her hand in mine. "I brought you something." I put the little blue angel in her hands.

"My guardian angel. Thank you, honey. She'll watch over me." She smiled and handed me the angel back. "Put it on the tray by my bed."

I did as she asked, happy that she embraced it in such a positive way. It had been my experience that creating positive thoughts helped to create wellness in people who were sick or in pain. The guardian angel was a way to give my grandmother hope and to make her feel comfort. We stayed awhile and promised to return to visit her the next day.

On my visit the following day, I discovered they had moved her to a semiprivate room on the third floor of the hospital. We took the elevator up and arrived to find my grandmother still somewhat alert, but now on morphine for the pain. She rambled on about different recipes and talked of times past. I looked around her and suddenly noticed that the angel was missing. One of my cousins inquired at the front desk, but they said no angel figurine was brought up when they moved Mama from the emergency room.

When we asked about the angel, we were told everything was sent up with Mama, but no one remembered. I took this as a sign that the little blue angel was meant for the person who was now in possession of it. Case closed.

When I arrived for my next visit, the room was filled with cousins, grandchildren, and my uncle, Mama's son. Busy greeting family with a kiss and a hug, it was several moments before I made my way over to the bed where Mama quietly slept. I took her hand and looked over at the machine that was sustaining her, when my eyes rested on something blue. I leaned closer and did a double take. The blue angel sat perched on the end table beside the bed!

I felt a hand on my shoulder. "We don't know how she got here, Linda. No one we have asked here seems to know anything about it. She just showed up."

I smiled. "Well, I guess she is meant to be here after all."

Faced with what was to become a weeklong death-watch, I drove back and forth to the hospital, each time feeling Mama was going to die any moment. As the week drew to a close, my grandmother drew her last breath. I was home when I received the call from my cousin.

"Mama died in her sleep. We're making arrangements." He went on to detail where the funeral would be held and discussed with me what color dress to buy. "One thing we really wanted," my cousin added, "was for you to have that little blue angel."

"What do you mean?" I had been sitting outside on the deck, enjoying the warm summer day. "What about the angel?" A loud noise came through the telephone, followed by static. "Wait, let me switch channels." I hit a few buttons and held the phone closer to my ear. "You were saying?"

"That little blue angel you gave her was not with the body when Mama was picked up from the hospital, and it wasn't with the personal items that were returned to us. We really thought you would have liked to have it as something to remember her by."

"It's okay," I said, once again accepting divine intervention. "Obviously, she is meant to be with someone else. Maybe her purpose is done now that Mama is gone," I reasoned aloud.

Three days later, Sue and I attended the wake that was held for Mama. My uncle had put together a memory board in the entrance: a special place for photos of Mama and the family through the years. Next to that was the guest book. We signed in and made our way over to the coffin. We were kneeling down side by side. Someone commented on how "good" Mama looked. (I have heard that compliment before at wakes and always thought it strange to say someone looked "good" when they had obviously been dead of the physical body for some three days and thus had to be preserved artificially.)

I gave a single nod and with a sign of the cross, bowed my head in prayer. Several minutes later, I slowly looked up. Almost in unison, Sue looked up with me. My eyes moved to my grandmother's head and were drawn to the opened coffin lid. A breath caught in my throat. There in the soft white folds inside the coffin lid was the blue angel! That deserves punctuation because it is the single most defining event in my life that proves beyond a shadow of a doubt that those in the afterlife communicate with us in a way that moves objects. At that very moment I knew that this was no ordinary angel. This angel was a messenger, and the spirit who was sending the message was my mother! It was suddenly so clear!

As soon as this realization hit me, it must have hit Sue because she stared straight at it, eyes wide open in mixed emotion. She noted the shock that was registered on my face and looked even more confused. (It never ceases to amaze me how people assume that because I am a practicing psychic medium that I am used to the surprising elements that may happen in life from a paranormal angle. Let the record show that I am always surprised and always delighted at every new discovery. Shocked, even, because it is all validation, and that validation, when recorded with oneself, is the most impressive of confirmations one can have.)

"Again, I don't know what to say." My cousin had tapped me on the shoulder and then bent to kiss my cheek. "The funeral director thought we'd be upset. They didn't put it there—"

"I know," I interrupted. "It's okay. It's really okay." I rose from my knees, and we walked over to mingle with those who were offering condolences.

The day Mama was buried, my uncle had asked me if I minded if they buried the blue angel with her. Before I could answer, my cousin deadpanned, "I don't think we have a choice. She's going whether we like it or not!" The comment brought a smile to my lips.

Chapter Thirty

BREAKING ON THROUGH TO
THE OTHER SIDE

····································

**Dedicated to Christian Russo: Earth Angel
Opening as a Medium for Others**

O N SEPTEMBER 11, 2001, fifteen minutes before
the Twin Towers in Manhattan were hit, and
five crucial seconds before I was to go on live radio for *The Cosmo Show* on WKGRS in Burlington, Iowa,
I knocked over the glass of water that was sitting on my
desk. I watched the clear liquid spread quickly over my
paperwork, making the ink a blue blotchy mess. I sighed.
Water spills have never been a good sign for me.

In the past, whenever I had made a particularly dis-
tressing psychic forecast or calculation, or when something personal and life changing was about to happen,
something would occur regarding water. A toilet would
overflow, pipes would burst, cups would spill over, and
so on. (Hurricane Floyd easily springs to mind!) I didn't
have to be a psychic to see the pattern and determine
water mishaps to be a "sign" of questionable news.

Readjusting my headphones, I quickly sopped up the water with a paper towel and tried to settle back in. The feeling of distress stayed with me, however, and I wasn't sure how to read it. Was it real distress or the usual butterflies I got whenever I was about to go on air? I was hoping that when Cosmo came on the feeling would go away, and I could dismiss it as pre-show jitters.

A disc jockey in the Midwest, Cosmo Leone was affiliated with Mix/KGRS in Burlington, Iowa, as program director and a radio personality with his own show. A real easy person to talk to, there was a spark between us from the start. I had been doing his show once a month for a year and had come to look forward to our light banter while doing the on-air readings of his listeners. (We would share a decade of insightful shows before his retirement from radio.)

This morning, Cosmo made his usual opening comments as we discussed current events and entertainment news on air before taking callers. As the negative feeling intensified, everything I was hearing had urgency to it. I found it extremely difficult to concentrate, and I just couldn't seem to put my finger on what was wrong. I talked about "warring" and the need for peace. I spoke about being calm and how important that was going to be in the coming days. To listen to an audiotape of that show today, you would think I knew something ahead of time but wasn't telling. The truth of the matter is that I didn't have anything more than a negative "feeling" and a spilled glass of water as a heads-up. The feeling had been with me for weeks. The water spilling just confirmed it all.

In the months that followed, I concentrated on reaching out to family, friends, and clients in an effort to help them process this tragedy. I held prayer meetings at my office to pray for the easy transition of the souls who perished, and I offered free guidance and information to those family members who needed grief counseling. The stress of this time made the days feel long and draining, and I recharged myself often through regular sessions of meditation. It was after one of these meditations that I had a dream in which I was surrounded by the energy of many spirits who were vying for my attention. Men and women unknown to me were moving their lips and reaching out with their hands in an attempt to speak to me. I couldn't hear what they were saying. At some point during the dream, I heard an orchestra of confusing melodies all blending together, and then one of the songs separated itself from the group. It was "Smooth," the Grammy-winning song by Carlos Santana and Rob Thomas. I knew the song, but it held no particular personal meaning for me. The dream left me with the song in my head and a strange longing to know the identity of the people and how I might communicate with them.

I began to experience this same dream many times over the next two months, with the song playing in my head in a continuous loop. One night one person separated himself from the others in the dream. A man in his mid-twenties who stood about five-eleven, with brown hair, came forward. I got the impression that he was the spokesperson for the other people in the dream. He also appeared to be responsible for the song that now played in my head so often that I wished I'd never heard it in the first place. I had never seen him before, yet his energy was strong enough to single him out from the others. When he spoke to me in the dream, it was with his eyes, and what he said remained with me when I woke up the next morning. He told me that others would be coming forward, and they all had messages that needed to be delivered.

Though the dreams themselves eventually stopped, the visions of the people continued, particularly the young man. I began to see flashes of these visitors in reading sessions, while I was writing, and even distracting me when I was shopping or driving. I never felt completely alone in a room, and I was forever having songs just pop into my head without obvious rhyme or reason. I found myself singing those songs, most times knowing all the words to a tune I had never heard before. I began to feel overwhelmed at being surrounded with all that unidentified energy with no outlet for it. It was a little like being in a crowded movie theater, trying to watch the movie while hearing every single separate conversation going on around you. It was unnerving. Something had to be done.

I reached out to Sue and our new business associate, Todd Evans, and asked them how I should resolve this problem. Sue suggested I open myself up to a larger forum. Doing so could possibly raise my chances of delivering some of the messages I was getting. It would also be a means for me to add to, and further work with, the symbols in my growing intuitive dictionary in an effort to decipher the messages more clearly. This sounded like a good idea. I was pretty sure the people in my dreams would not let me down, since they were the ones who initiated this in the first place.

The most important technique I use in working with the energy of those who passed on is translating messages from them by way of my own familiar frames of reference. For instance, I might see a flash of John Travolta or John Lennon and interpret this as a spirit's way of telling me that his name is John. Other times, I might see the image of my mother, which could mean I was tapping into the late mother of the person I was reading; or I might smell the aroma of fresh-baked cookies, which might indicate the person's name (Cookie) or perhaps hobby (baking cookies). How I translated it made all the difference. Mistakes are as easily made in this spiritual language, as they are between any two people with different dialects.

The people on the other side show you whatever they can to get your attention and sustain it long enough to send a message. Songs, cartoons, people, relatives, and personal memories are all means by which they accomplished this. Anything might be used. Over time, I had developed a dictionary of symbols and definitions to learn to understand and speak this new language. I worked with the other side through a kind of spiritual shorthand in pictures.

My introductions always came through direct invitation via an object, picture, signature, or anything that had their energy on it. Once I secured this invitation, I would get a strong sense of actual energy blocking the area to the left of me, and I would become aware that someone was indeed sitting next to me. A picture that related to that person's life in some way immediately followed, and as soon as that connection was established, I would hear, see, smell, and sense things that pertained to the person's life. It would be up to whomever I was doing the reading for to validate what I was saying.

To do this on a larger scale, Sue rented a meeting room at one of the local Hilton hotels and advertised a "Psychic Evening of Audience Readings" for the next month. We decided to limit the audience to fifty people this first time. After that we would review and tweak the number if necessary. When I look back on that first Psychic Evening now, I can't believe I was still physically standing at the end. I felt drained by the group of fifty people, especially with the energy of fifty more people tapping into me from the other side. It took me two weeks to recover physically.

Creating the right atmosphere for an event that is spiritually directed is very important. I wanted the room to have an angel figurine or two next to some flowers. I debated over whether we needed music, whether I wanted to use a microphone, and whether I would ask other people to help me get the "invitations" from the audience. Todd offered to help out for the evening. A spiritual student of mine, Todd was in the position to anticipate my needs because he was familiar with how I did my work. I knew too that his positive energy would prove an asset to the eventual success of the evening.

My stomach started to do little flip-flops as I entered our meeting room in the Hilton for the first Psychic Evening. Booking the event had been easy, but anything is possible when communicating with spirit, and I was feeling apprehensive. We were in one of the larger meeting rooms, where we had our own bathroom and the luxury of a separate room that normally held the bar. It is always important for me to have quiet time for prayer and meditation prior to doing any psychic work. I chose the little bar as the place to sequester myself for my prep time, because I couldn't see out and no one could see in. The CD player I'd brought along prevented me from hearing any of the conversations as people arrived, while also serving to provide soft music for the waiting audience.

As Sue attended to the details of setup in the main room, I stole into the bar with my little black case and closed the door behind me. The case contained everything I needed to create a sacred space—things that were representative of the little altar I had at home. The suitcase contained a scarf, a small angel figurine, a small amethyst cluster, a votive candle and holder, incense with a burner, and my mother's Holy Rosary. My little suitcase offered nourishment for my spirit, and I was grateful.

Once everything was laid out and the candle was lit, I turned down the lights and sat back into the chair to pray for guidance for the evening. My heart hammered in my chest as I heard people taking their seats in the main room, no one having a clue that I was sequestered nearby. We had a full house, and I could feel that the energy in the room was high. Soon Sue introduced me.

The soft scent of sandalwood incense blended with the sweetness of carnations as I walked up to the front of the audience. I took a deep breath and smiled. I could literally feel my angels around me. I gave the audience the rundown on how the evening would go and explained that I made no promises as to who was brought through and hoped that they left their expectations at the door. I explained that communication would be by their invitation, not mine. I considered myself a translator. Their loved ones would come to them before they would to a stranger, and it was important to keep that in mind.

Todd dimmed the lights, and Sue turned the soft music up a little louder as I led the audience through a guided meditation for about ten minutes. It must have connected them in some way, because I could feel the vibration in the room change as the group slowly came out of it. This was a good sign, as I believed that the success of the evening would rely heavily on the collective energy of the audience members. The stronger they were together, the easier it would be for me to work. This was a group experience, and if even one person had a wall up in some way, they could easily ruin it for the rest.

I finished the meditation, and Todd lowered the music as the group opened their eyes. My focus was immediately drawn to a blonde-haired woman in one of the back rows on the right side of the room. I sent Todd over to her seat to get her invitation. He came back with a picture of a short, white-haired woman in her eighties who was blowing out the candles on a birthday cake. I looked down at her face and then back up again to the woman in the audience, and in an instant felt a warm, soft energy standing beside me.

"This is your grandmother," I confirmed.

"Yes," the woman said in response.

"She is showing me a wall sampler…a family sampler. Do you understand this?"

"Yes," she replied, her eyes fast filling up with tears.

"I'm getting the name Helen or Ellen…" I felt intense heat beside me and quickly confirmed, "Helen. She wants me to say Helen."

"Yes!" The woman started to cry, letting her tears fall freely.

I walked down the aisle to offer her comfort as the audience switched around in their seats for a better view of what was transpiring.

The young woman pulled her sweater tightly around her as if to ward off a chill. "I'm just so happy to know she's here." She dabbed at her eyes with a tissue. "I have the sampler."

"But you don't have it hanging up," I said. "She's showing me my basement, so I sense that Helen's sampler is packed away somewhere…"

"That's right. I just moved into a new apartment and haven't had time to unpack it. I was debating about where to put it."

"The kitchen. She's showing me a kitchen."

"That's where she hung it when she was alive."

"Then that's where you should put it." I patted the young woman's shoulder.

"Whenever you see that sampler, please be reminded that she's with you."

When I touched her, I instantly felt her grandmother's energy leave my side, and I understood this to mean the message had been delivered. I was now being directed to a nice-looking man across the room.

I walked over and said a hello. His name was Lou, and he handed me his invitation—a man's wallet. When I touched it, I got the flash of a smile that I thought was very familiar. I had seen that smile before and knew this energy. I moved the wallet around in my hands for more information. Unfortunately, I couldn't quite tune into much more than that, and I wasn't feeling any energy manifest to my side to identify the owner of the wallet.

"Can I keep this up front for a bit?" I asked. Lou nodded in agreement. "I'm not feeling a strong enough connection right this moment, but I hope to be able to do so later."

I moved to the front and put the wallet on the table, my attention now on a woman in her late sixties who was seated in the second row.

"The lady in the flowered blouse," I told Todd as I pointed to her. My senses suddenly filled with the scent of fresh roses, and at the same time the image of them flashed inside my head. "Rose...I can smell them, and I can see them. Rose is here." With that acknowledgement came the presence of energy, and I could feel Rose's motherly vibration at my side.

Todd handed me a photograph, and as he did, the woman stood up. "Rose is my mother-in-law."

"She raised prize-winning roses," interjected the man beside her, Rose's son.

I moved with my microphone back over to my chair and sat down. "She's very pleased by what you've done with the living room." I shook my head a little at the kind of details the afterlife picked up and smiled at the couple. "She also likes the altar that you've set up in her memory. She particularly likes the sculpture of the angel."

The audience was riveted, and several people said that they, too, could smell roses in the room. Rose's son and daughter-in-law were delighted by the validation they were receiving. The message went on mostly about family, but Rose's primary concern was that they, the family, continue to use and pass on her Italian recipes. Apparently, her son had the collection and was putting together a book for family members and was already doing this.

I moved all over the audience that evening, gravitating from the energy of one person to another. This group was "hot" in that they were able to synchronize their focus as a group and therefore stir up a great deal of positive energy. Positive energy creates a higher vibration, which is what I find is necessary to communicate with those who have died. Each one of us contributes our own unique energy to a place when we enter it. One light will illuminate a corner, but a chandelier can illuminate an entire room. My audience was a lot like a chandelier, creating energy enough to illuminate the messages the other side was sending. Their collective energy would always garner the best results.

As I continued, I felt like a tennis ball being lobbed back and forth between the energy on this side and the energy of the other. It took a while for me to ground myself while trying to keep up with the information and the people coming through, but I was completely enjoying it. I kept being pulled over to Lou and the wallet, but then nothing would happen, and I would be pulled to another person in the room instead. After several more readings, I was once again pulled over to the wallet. I picked it up and walked around the room with it in my hand, my concentration now on a woman in the audience who showed me a picture of her husband.

A decidedly male energy made its presence known, but he seemed reluctant to stake claim as to who he was. I felt a sudden shift of vibration from across the room to where Lou was sitting. Instead of acknowledging this, I stayed with the woman. This time, I was resonating strongly with the energy.

"Who is Chris?" I asked confidently.

The woman shrugged her shoulders and took the picture from my hand. "My husband's name is not Chris!" she replied indignantly. "And he's not dead," she continued. "I just want to know when the hell he's going to die so that I'm rid of him!"

Before I could say anything, Lou spoke up from his seat across the room. "That's him. Chris. My son is Chris! He's the owner of the wallet."

Like a gentle hand on my shoulder, Chris's energy firmly wrapped itself around me, and it was the strongest energy I had felt since the evening began. This was all the confirmation I needed as I stepped over to where Lou was sitting, Chris's wallet "talking" to me with each step.

"This was sudden…unexpected. He was alone."

"Yes." Lou leaned forward and handed me a photograph. "This is one of the last pictures."

I looked down at what was in his hands. Chris had been in his twenties when he died. "He's showing me water…a stream. He's not sure how this happened because it was so fast. I'm getting the impression of someone falling over. As if he was walking near a body of water, lost consciousness, and fell in. It all happened very quickly…suddenly. I feel it may have been precipitated by an impact in the chest area. Unexpected. It was an accident." I paused a few moments before handing the wallet back to Lou. "And he accepts that it was supposed to happen. Chris has more to do where he is in terms of guiding others. His work is only beginning."

Lou leaned back into the chair. "That sounds just like Chris. He would be the first to help other people who needed him." Lou took the wallet back and shifted a little. "We're really not sure what happened to Chris. They found him behind the neighbor's property, laying face down in a small brook that had only a few inches of water in it."

"Please know that Chris is always with you and saw this opportunity as a way to let you know that," I said as I prepared to move on to the next reading. I thought that when I handed the wallet back over to Lou that Chris would leave, as that action should have completed his message. Chris, however, did not plan on going anywhere just yet and had much more he wanted to say. I jokingly explained to the audience they we would have to entertain Chris for a little while longer, and no one seemed to mind. In fact, the reverse was true, as they were enjoying the fact that their energy was a part of the reason why this experience was happening at all. There was an unexplainable amount of energy that charged the room with excitement.

That's when it hit me: the song I had been hearing those months earlier in my dreams came back hauntingly familiar and loud in my head now. It was so distracting that I became dizzy for a moment. Now I knew why Chris's energy was so familiar to me. The song belonged to him. He was the visitor who had set himself apart from the others in my dream those months ago! The spokesperson was finally here. I would finally be able to help him.

"I can't believe I didn't connect this before," I said as I paced back up to the front again. "'Smooth,'" I said, looking over at Lou.

"'Smooth,'" Lou confirmed as his eyes misted over. "Carlos Santana. The song 'Smooth' from the *Supernatural* CD was Chris's favorite song," he said in a choked voice.

I explained to the audience that for a long time I had been dreaming about the other side, and in those dreams I kept hearing that same song. "Now I know where that sign belongs, with Chris." I turned back to Lou again. "He's fine. You must try to understand that. He wants me to tell you that he is completely free now. He needs for you to believe and trust that there was nothing you or anyone could have changed to prevent him from dying when he did."

I felt Chris pull his energy slightly away, but he still seemed to linger. In fact, like an invisible force, he guided my vision over to a young woman in the audience who couldn't have been more than nineteen or twenty.

"Todd, the young woman in the red blouse," I said, pointing to the back of the room.

Todd came back with a picture of two very pretty teenage girls. The brunette was the young woman in the audience. Chris was showing me pictures of the other young woman sitting alone in her room, crying. He showed me a drawer of drugs that were mostly prescription. The last image he flashed was of a funeral.

"This is a suicide," I said.

The young woman sat back down into her seat and drew a tissue from her pocket. "Yes. She was my best friend."

As soon as she confirmed this, I felt the girl's energy settle in beside Chris and me. "She knows you tried to prevent this from happening. She wants you to stop blaming yourself. She is pointing to herself. She accepts full responsibility for what she did."

"She doesn't hate me for not being there?" she asked, fresh tears building up in her eyes.

"Of course not." All at once I felt warmth literally flush my body. "In fact, she loved you very much," I said, confirming that feeling out loud.

"Thank you. Thank you so much."

"We have Chris to thank for your friend's visit. He showed me the way by escorting your friend through this process."

When I looked over to Lou and smiled, I could feel Chris's energy finally pull back and away for the evening. But that was not Chris's only Psychic Evening. He continued to visit and bring others through on some of the subsequent evenings that followed, particularly if he had family in the audience. He was one of those energies I came to count on. He was a spiritual assistant to me, and I am grateful to Chris and happy that I was able to make that connection for him. The fact that he makes that connection for others further instills my faith in the delivery and receipt of the messages I continue to receive daily. I had never come across a spirit as evolved or as strong as Chris. His mission was clearly to help others to communicate. The dreams prepared me for his assistance, as I had not experienced an unknown spirit in a dream prior to a client's reading before or since. Chris's desire to help, coupled with his sincerity to get a message to his family, was unique.

All in all, the evening was considered a success, and while Sue packed up the main room with Todd, I packed up my portable sacred space, and then we headed home. I came away from that evening with a profound respect for those who have died for continuing to communicate, as well as a deep gratitude to those on this side who choose to be open enough to actually receive and participate in that heavenly dialog.

* * *

Each day, I am discovering ways that nourish me rather than deprive me of spiritual communication. It feels good. Warm. I am being offered and am offering to others a richer experience as I pick up more signs and actually formulate a cohesive message! Trust me, there is nothing in the world like it.

Chapter Thirty-One

LINDA LAUREN'S ENERGY ART™

....

W HAT IF IT were possible to harness the colors of your aura and work with them in a visual way that would produce a positive intention? Well, it is very possible, and it is the result of deep meditation on my part to work with the color and energy of my clients in a way that would be beneficial to them by connecting the energy of body and mind with spirit.

Our aura/energy field is affected by the energy of the colors we surround ourselves and come in contact with. Color is the reason why you feel happy, sad, sick, or well. It's why red may represent love while it might also represent rage. Green can embrace money, but it can also heal matters of the heart, literally and figuratively. We are a clean canvas, and we can paint ourselves a rainbow of motivation or paint ourselves into a corner of depression. Color matters to our mood, and I work with the aura through meditation and intention to create art that reveals what will be most beneficial to your spirit. It's art to make you feel good, and when we feel good, we attract even more good. I guess you could say I'm working with your aura via the law of attraction through color and your own vital energy!

All this just happened one night when I was alone at the computer. I am a technical junkie, and I love to learn anything new in that department. I'm an Apple person and love my Macs and iPads and, to that end, worked with at least four different art programs until I developed a proprietary way to create this new form of art. My first attempts were the same as the others I had earlier when developing products. I felt a hand over mine, and after meditating and holding a recent photo of the person in my mind (and on my computer), my fingers moved the mouse and dipped into the colors to create swirls of light, color, and voids to fill. I *loved* this process, and it made me feel good to make others feel good! There was only one thing missing: a translation. It's important for people to know what something means so they can utilize it to their best advantage. So each piece came with a translation, and before I knew it, I was having an art show in Chelsea in NYC that became a media event.

Gratitude is limitless in my world, and I have gone as far as to do Human Rights Campaign events, as well as donating the art for auction. And the techie in me went a step further and opened up the positive energy by creating an app that expresses the artwork along with a translation in a way that allows you to be part of the process. You just pick a card and hold on to the positive colors and words described. I decided to call it The Vibe™ of Linda Lauren's Energy Art™. If you'd like, head over to iTunes and check it out!

Chapter Thirty-Two

THE CENTER OF IT ALL!

··

A ROUND 2005, AFTER researching a couple of different locations, we decided to look for a storefront to open up our new business. Sue and I exhausted ourselves in search of the right space in the right town for the right price. We settled on a storefront with a lot of light and potential that would afford us retail as well as private spaces for me to conduct classes and private reading sessions. We set about ordering for the space and had our partner, Todd, come by to check it out before signing the lease. Everything was in order, and we were enthusiastic about this new venture!

At noon on the day of our move, we had packed up a portable sacred space to take along with us while we set up the business. That's when the phone rang, and when I say Sue and I were literally almost out the door with cleaning supplies, inventory, and our sacred space, I mean it. She ran back to answer it and quickly put it on speaker so we could both hear.

"I am so sorry," our attorney was saying. "Apparently there is a law on the books dating to 1996 that indicates your line of work is not permitted in that city."

He paused. "I don't know what to say, except that it's ridiculous, and I'm sorry this happened to you."

I was devastated. I come from the "If you build it, they will come" school of thought, and this was just totally unacceptable, yet there was nothing we could do about it. That is when the phone rang again, proving my mother's theory that "For every down, there is an up." It was our friend and business associate, Todd. He was thrilled to have finished work on the offices he had just remodeled. His business was lodged in the historic Smith-Williams House, built in 1790 in the town of Mountainside, New Jersey. Despite the fact that he was remodeling it for office space, he was very careful and considerate in keeping the building's historic integrity intact, right down to the wording of the plaque on the building.

"We just finished laying down the carpeting in the lower level suite. It looks fantastic. Now all I have to do is rent it! But, how are you doing? Isn't today the big moving day?"

Tears welled up in my eyes, and I told him the whole story. I could hear him laughing on the other end, and I could not believe he was doing that!

"What is so funny about us not having a place to work from for our clients? I don't want to work from home—"

"I'm laughing because you do have a place to go! Would you consider relocating to Mountainside? You can be close by, and the office space needs a tenant. Come over and have a look. It couldn't hurt, right?"

"It couldn't hurt."

Linda Lauren's Embracing The Universe moved into 1248 Route 22 West in Mountainside in November of 2005. Every single room in our gorgeous center was designed by angelic collaboration. I can recall standing in the middle of the empty rooms and "seeing" what would go there and where we might get it. A lot of my reading room furniture is antique and family heirlooms, but in a way that nourishes! We have five rooms that include a healing room, with crystals, jewelry, and candles; an office; a reception area; and my own reading room, which is a haven and a foundation for me to feel secure. We also have an art gallery that we created for classes, lectures, group and art events.

The building itself is haunted, and I, as well as others, have experienced some pretty intense things going on. Pens have gone flying, shadows have moved, and I have seen a woman at a stove on the third floor. She was cooking. Her name is Evelyn, but there is no real stove there, and no woman was actually cooking. She was a momentary vision, and one I have seen on more than one occasion. She is like a guardian to our space.

The Center is a blessing. We have had angel figurines move on their own, songs play messages that only we would understand, and people whispering when we are obviously alone. But there is no fear, because we are love. The building is love, and our establishment is love. To visit The Center is to embrace love in a way that is universal, and we strive to include the spirits into that family.

Chapter Thirty-Three

PET PSYCHIC

....

THE PREVIOUS YEAR, someone approached me in my business network to write a column for a new publication that was to be called *The New York Dog Magazine*, with the promise of the column being carried over to a West Coast version, *The Hollywood Dog Magazine*. I have had pets all my life, mostly dogs, and have learned to communicate with them intuitively and telepathically. The magazines were glossy, social, and very upscale in photography and stories. My column, Psychic Companion™ was picked up by them. It explored past life connections with people and their pets. Those publications are now out of circulation, but I still have the column via my own site. Pet consultations are also still a part of my practice today via Skype.

The exposure got Psychic Companion™ noticed and written about by the *Chicago Tribune* and other news media outlets. I soon began to do fund-raisers with my dog at the time, a Jack Russell terrier named Ginger. I met some wonderful pets and felt good about the work I was doing and the help I was giving.

At one point during all of this animal activity, the BBC contacted me to inquire about filming me at my metaphysical center for a "dogumentary" they were producing in Ireland. They wanted an interview, and they wanted to film the center during a pet reading with one of the producers. We set up a time and date and arranged for them to come with cameras and crew in tow.

They arrived early in the day and focused their cameras in my reading room, around the table. I sat at the table, but rather than put my Ginger on my lap, they gave me Sue's little dog, Cosmo, and Sue sat to the left of me with Ginger. Maybe they thought this would be a test for my abilities; I'm not sure. All I know is that energy is everywhere and every person, place, and thing can be read. They began filming, and I immediately sensed an energy in the room. I had a feeling that they would be filming Sue and Cosmo, so I purposely asked Sue not to tell me of her questions beforehand so as to keep it fresh and spontaneous.

They loved the vibe in The Center, which only made for a more interesting feeling to the shoot. It had softer energy and was less hectic than they were used to.

Once they were camera ready, and the wireless mics were in place, Sue asked me about what she referred to as Cosmo's "Dumpster diving." At the time, he would go into the trash. He looked up at me with his round, dark eyes, and I "saw" a ball. He told me he was looking for his pink rubber ball that was tossed in a previous life. He said he keeps going into trash containers to get his favorite toy back but can't find it. I recommended getting him that ball and putting it in the bottom of a trashcan. Then she could take it out in front of Cosmo, so he would now see it as if he's gotten it back! A little paranormal slight of hand!

I tapped into his previous lives and to that of Ginger's, when suddenly, in the middle of Cosmo's reading, he started a low growl and stared hard at Quinn, the director. I tried to quiet him, but he would not stop. His focus went down to the floor beside Quinn, and I looked there, too. I told Quinn that there was an older woman with dark hair and a little white dog; did he know her or the dog? I asked him again several times and still didn't get a response. He stood stunned and called for a break but said, "Continue filming." I asked him to please validate it, and he nodded his head yes. I asked if the name of the dog was like "Tigger" or something that started with a *T*. Quinn finally said he knew the lady and the dog, Tito. At this point Cosmo stopped growling, and the validation was completed. We continued to film, and Quinn related to us that the dog had recently passed away and was attached to him and belonged to his aunt.

As the session continued, the camera changed angles and the "kids" continued to talk more. Ginger and Cosmo, we learned, had spent many lifetimes together and knew each other well.

An hour and fifteen minutes later, we were done. They took some exterior shots and thanked us before leaving. They were a great group of people. They were respectful, thoughtful, and when they left, the place looked like they never were there, because they put everything back in place in the room.

New LLETU Logo

Spirit Orbs

Guardian Angel

Linda's Reading Room

Psychic Evening of Audience Readings

Linda and Ginger

Gidget

Chapter Thirty-Four

THE MEDIUM AND THE MONKEE

....

W HEN MY THIRTY-YEAR high school reunion came around, I never expected to hook up with someone who would be able to extend my reach in my career so that I could meet more people. But I found that person in my high school friend Bruce Goldberg. As it turned out, Bruce (known as "Brucer, the Producer") was now producing the *Micky in the Morning* radio show on the then popular WCBS-FM in New York.

This was an early morning drive to New York gig, but we really loved doing it. I love the radio because it connects me to the voice, and the voice carries energy that is very different than sight for me. I am able to catch what I can only explain as "multiple whispers"—sounds/ voices that are caught via transmitter or signal, saying something that may (if I'm lucky) actually offer me snippets of information. Sort of like a human version of an EMF meter that some of us use in paranormal investigation. And often on Micky's show we would have some incredible experiences with the callers.

My first live show started out jovial and a lot of fun, and Bruce was (and still is) a great producer. I was tickled to see him again and to meet Micky and the crew. Micky gave me a signed copy of his book. I did a piece of personalized Linda Lauren's Energy Art™ just for his vibration as a gift in return.

While I adjusted my headphones, Micky told me briefly about his interest in metaphysics and personal experiments he did in the 60s and 70s with telekinesis. He meditated back in the day and had a belief system. Soon, the ON AIR light blinked. All gave a thumbs-up, and we were off and running with some banter. Up until now I had done live radio via telephone, so I enjoyed being next to them in the studio where I could help create the collective "team" vibe I knew was necessary for people to harmonize on radio as a group. The banter had to be good to keep people listening. Though Micky opened up with a spooky kind of music for my appearance, he suddenly asked his engineer to cut the music the moment we started to talk on air. For me, that was the most respectful way anyone has ever treated me. It was easy to take teasing from Micky, because he's genuine and authentic, and when he recognizes other people who share that, he is quick to be an ally.

We took a few calls, joked about how just the day before Mick Jagger or Rod Stewart or some such rocker had been in the very seat I was now sitting in, and then went to commercial break. While the callers were lined up, Micky and I had a brief chat about Laurel Canyon in California back in the day. I shared with him the fact that Jim Morrison (of The Doors) had been a friend, and he shared that he had lived in the canyon at that same time. We shared a memory but were soon back to the live feed.

As we took the calls, Micky was very cordial and sweet, and I did my best to engage callers by giving each a quick read on their vibe to fit as many calls in as short a time as possible. The first few calls were about relationships, and we were all having some fun with them, when the next caller before break came on. She had lost a loved one, and there were a few nanoseconds of dead air as the control booth went quiet. Dead air is not a good thing in radio, but I could tell that everyone was taken aback at the unexpected turn.

I remember Micky leaning forward into the microphone and extending his condolences, at a loss as to how he might handle this. Before he could look to me, I began talking, and the energy of this young woman's loved one came through. Though I was under controlled conditions, with about a minute or so to go before I would be cut off, I was trying to give this woman her message before I lost the caller for the closing of the show. There hadn't been enough time to prepare for the unexpected, so none of us thought to take down any names and numbers. I finished speaking and looked up at the engineer who mouthed "Wow" just as Micky said the word to me. The caller was gone, and they were closing the show, but not before he invited me back to continue as his Resident Psychic.

WCBS-FM's morning broadcast on June 3, 2005, was a remote at a nightclub/restaurant called BB King's to celebrate Micky's one-hundredth day at the station. The invitations were limited, and as his Resident Psychic for the show, I was invited.

We sat at a table up front, close to the main DJ remote table in case Micky wanted me to come up. Micky and his band put on a great show, and so did the other singers who are now a blur. It was loud, it was fun, and it was unfortunately a good-bye performance that no one saw coming. By the end of that day, the station would be changed dramatically by a hostile takeover. It was the last morning broadcast.

Chapter Thirty-Five

YOU SAID GOOD-BYE, BUT I'LL SAY HELLO!

. . . .

O N T H E A F T E R N O O N of June 23, 2006, my world changed when Ginger was hit by a car after having been "spooked" out of her leash. The day she was killed by an uncaring driver who did not stop will remain deep within my spirit, and it chipped a bit of me away.

I was not present when it happened, but about three minutes before the call came, I felt a sharp pain in the back of my head. The phone rang, and my friend, Sue, who had been walking her, called crying to say that a car backfired, Ginger got spooked, slipped out of her collar, and was hit by a car. She died instantly. The pain in my head went away and was replaced by tears.

I remember it like it was yesterday. I was wearing a T-shirt and jeans. The shirt was one of my funny ones. It read: *HELP! I'm talking and I can't shut up*. But that day it took on a new meaning as I stood by the open front door, plastered against it, the word *HELP* pleading people to see my pain. I tossed that shirt right afterward because it was a sore reminder of my Ginger. She was the last connection to my mother, and perhaps I held onto that so severely that it made Ginger's loss that much greater.

Though I wish she could have been with me for many more years, I know that we shared a bond that transcended any others in my life. Ginger gave me so much healing after my mother's death that I prospered personally and professionally, and I instinctively "knew" that she was my "psychic companion."

I came to the understanding and realization that her passing was not the choice of God and the universe. It was her own choice of panic, and that is the reason she is not with us today. Even animals make choices that are beyond our protection. What I knew for sure at the time was that she was only a vibration away, and I would sense her again through another pet. Until then, I tried to keep the light in my heart from dimming by recharging through prayer and by being open to the signs.

On the third day after Ginger's passing, I took a trip to the ocean to clear my head. I asked her to give me a sign that she was okay. While walking along the sand trail in Hazlet, New Jersey, and back to the car, my eyes rested on the ground. Right by my foot was a small, perfectly shaped white feather. Here was my sign! I picked it up and slipped it into my wallet alongside Ginger's picture.

I was plagued with dreams—strong, intense dreams with Ginger romping—and I began to have the same dream of her over and over. In the dreams, she introduced me to an all-white female puppy that reminded me of both a Maltese and a poodle, a combination I had never heard of. This was one of those times I could have used my mother's Dream Lady help, but, as a medium I did take this as a sign. I shared the dreams with no one and waited for more signs. Shortly thereafter, a friend stopped by with a small gift to help me through the nights without Ginger. It was a white stuffed animal that looked remarkably like the puppy in my dreams.

The next morning, I came across e-mail correspondence from a stranger announcing "Malti-Poo Puppies for Sale." The location was Hazlet, New Jersey—the same exit as the beach where I found Ginger's first sign to me of the white feather.

These signs were coming fast and in succession, so I gave the breeder a call. It was more a case of two dogs who got loose and one got pregnant. They didn't know what to do with all the puppies. They had two females and a male left from a litter of six. They were white with a little cream on each ear and on top of the head. I got directions and made an appointment to visit. When I told my friend about it, she said, "You're going to travel an hour's drive? Don't be disappointed if you don't come home with your little girl." But my response was that I "knew" I would be bringing home my new dog. And Sue was good at giving me the signal that we should discuss it before purchase. She would signal me to "talk about it over a cup of coffee." That was an easy translation. It meant: no way! And we'd be on to the next one.

The moment I arrived, one of the puppies ran up to me: a female. They were three months old, and she, in particular, looked remarkably like the dream puppy and similar to the stuffed animal! There was a lot of commotion and excitement, and the breeder called out to the puppy that greeted me. "We call her Petunia."

"Petunia?" Sue repeated in question and looked at me with a knowing smile.

The woman nodded as she juggled Petunia on her hip, over her very pregnant stomach. We both knew that was my next sign, as Petunia was the name my mother called me as a baby, and as my friend, Sue knew this story about me.

Later, Sue asked what I intended to name her. I looked at the date. It was July 22. I had been without a pet for almost a full month. Not long to some, but ages to a person who was grieving in a house with other pets belonging to a roommate. I loved them all, but I wanted a dog of my own.

As a fan of surfing and the Gidget books and movies, I knew that the real Gidget first surfed on July 22, 1958! That's what I named my new psychic companion: Gidget. Amazingly, upon arriving to her new home, she immediately dug into the bottom of Ginger's toy box, and out of the tons of squeaky toys, she carefully picked out a tiny piece of a toy ear that had been Ginger's favorite!

And the signs kept coming. To those of you who have lost your own little companion, please be open to signs. They are everywhere.

Chapter Thirty-Six

PARANORMAL INVESTIGATING WITH THE TEAM—JUST MAKE YOUR PRESENCE KNOWN!

···

O N MORE THAN one occasion, I have been asked to visit a building, home, or site because the owners were upset about repeated occurrences they believed to be a haunting. I am never quick to agree, because there are many things that come into play that can make one think they are in the presence of a ghost. There are also enough television shows out there that have left us with a pretty savvy audience. I don't mind people using the sophisticated and expensive equipment available to this relatively new field. What I do object to are the techniques some employ, like provocation. There is no reason to assume anything regarding what you might think you are experiencing when you are met with someone who may be dead. So much energy has "died" on the land being investigated that there is really no true way to ascertain that anyone was speaking to the person "assumed" to be haunting the place. I do not like the word "assume," because it goes against my entire intuitive nature. Basically, the rule of thumb on any investigation is to never assume and never provoke. I'm not talking about dark forces here. I'm speaking in terms of your everyday ghost haunting. Meaning that, in most cases, you are not provoking a dark force but someone's relative. You are trespassing on their property, not the other way around. Why would you disrespect the property of someone else, and why would you yell at a perfect stranger? That is what many novice or unseasoned paranormal investigators do, and to add insult to injury, they often discount real evidence simply because they have no other means to explain it. They give it all up too easily for the sake of the television cameras, and they don't communicate; yet they expect the spirit or ghost to do so. They walk around intuiting, yet they say they don't use psychics. This makes me shake my head because clearly there is a huge gap between the people who actually are mediums and those who are claiming to investigate the ghosts the mediums are communicating with.

There are only two people I have ever admired on any of the present shows who are respectfully communicating: Amy Bruni of *Ghost Hunters* and Meat Loaf (yes, the singer) when he made his *Ghost Hunters* appearance. They are two very talented mediums and communicators. They don't have to put a label on it. Just look at the results when Amy is using the flashlight as her "tool," or tune in to the episode where Meat Loaf has the spirit communicating with him like they were long-lost friends! He is an amazing medium, and he is right on when it comes to the words to use and the respect necessary to garnish results. This man doesn't need a dashboard to see the light. He knows it's there and how to relate to it.

There have been many times over the years that I have been called upon to help someone who wanted an explanation as to why they were uncomfortable in their homes. Often times I zoom straight for a particular antique they may have just acquired, with the knowledge that the source of the discomfort in the home was stemming from the particular item in question. Other times, I could pinpoint the source as not paranormal at all but a case of electrical wires or something more normal than paranormal.

I have investigated a lot of homes, establishments, and property, as well as cleared them and raised the vibration to be more positive. Sometimes, though, I might come across a really stubborn place, and all the clearing and cleansing I do just doesn't seem to make a positive difference. In those cases, I conduct a lengthy interview of the occupants or people involved, especially if there are teenagers in the house. Teens have the strongest energy, which can make for unreliable spikes in readings because they are at the high hormonal part of life, unlike children of five or six who are naïve and still very innocent and tap into spirit directly.

In cases where the above has been ruled out, I conduct a deeper investigation that incorporates the use of my intuition with camera and detection equipment as I read the color and energy vibration I am being met with.

One such instance concerned a family with two children who were experiencing depression. There were occurrences in the house that they felt threatened by, and they were looking for answers. It only took the first ten minutes of the house tour for me to realize what the problem was. Oh, they were being haunted—that's for sure. But it was self-created by residual energy that was playing itself out over and over through their ancestors via the multitude of photographs displayed in the home. We are not talking a few photos strategically placed. There was that, too, as well as rooms full of antiques dating back to the late 1700s. What greeted those who entered that house once they crossed the threshold was what was causing the most trouble. It made sense that the main question the owners had was why they had so much negativity when they tried to invite people into the house.

Additionally, they seemed to be quarrelling a lot, and the children were reporting shadow figures moving throughout the house that frightened them. The son was a teenager, and the daughter was about five years old. The boy was hearing things, too, and the little girl was holding entire conversations with an unseen person. As a child who had a "real" imaginary friend, I didn't judge what the little girl might have been seeing, and the boy was denying that anything was wrong or that he even saw anything.

My team now consisted of Sue, Todd, and Jeffrey Moran, whom I met through Todd. Jeffrey and I had done corporate seminars, as well as several investigations as a team. He is now on board as my Talent Manager.

It's important to note here that I had not done my first walk-through by way of the front door and had, instead, entered by way of the back door and the pool area. So basically, we saw the kitchen first. As we made our way through the foyer to the front door, I waited as my team took photos. It didn't take me long to figure out what the problem was. Yes, they were being haunted, but it was by their own invitation!

"When did you put those up?" I asked.

Crossing the foyer from the front door was a staircase that wound to the right. Above the banister and across the entire wall that faced the entryway were at least a hundred photographs covering every inch of wall space. All dated back to the nineteenth century, and each was in a frame from the time period that really belonged more in a museum than a home, and I said as much.

"What is this all about?" I asked before revealing my impression to the client.

"Those are my relatives." She darted a look to her husband, who stood silently next to her while she did all the talking. "They are *my* relatives, and they are there to protect me and keep me safe."

"The energy is extremely dense in the area from the door to the staircase. All you are doing is encouraging people *away* from you by displaying them this way." I touched a hand to a photograph of a man with a cigar. Pudgy, dressed wealthy, and not happy. In fact, that is what was so disturbing. No one was happy in the photos or in the house, and I was fast becoming depressed myself just being there.

"Let's move away from the wall and talk outside," the husband offered. "I hate that wall myself, and I agree with you. But my wife wants it that way."

We sat down on their patio as they served us lemonade. "Then I can't help you," I replied, taking a sip. "As long as those photographs from the past are up, you are inviting in energy that is not healthy to your family life in the present."

Before we left, I gave them a candle and told them to pray for protection and guidance, and I said I hoped she would reconsider changing that front wall. For a while, the husband still came to me for readings and told me that his wife had changed things. However, it may have been too late for this family to come back together, which upsets me when the solution was so very simple.

Chapter Thirty-Seven

EMBRACING THE METAVERSE— THE VIRTUAL MEDIUM

····································

W HAT KEPT ME entertained on those nights when I couldn't sleep were the multitude of podcasts that predates smartphones, tablets, and YouTube. Computer blogging was not as media driven, and entertainment came in the form of the video podcast. These little shows were innovative, fun, and informative, and I found myself on a few of the metaphysical ones as a guest on more than one occasion. I was supportive of the format, and there was always the potential for discovering new podcasts.

I have my favorites, among them *Tiki Bar TV, Geekbrief,* and *Diggnation.* I really enjoyed anything that was tech related, and it was the technical side of podcasts that got me involved in the virtual world of Second Life.

I was a of fan Cali Lewis's show (now called Geekbeat TV) and Alex Albrecht and Kevin Rose, who have since left Diggnation. There are others, but those particular three people stand out. It was actually Cali Lewis who inadvertently got me involved in the virtual world of

Second Life. I have her to thank for the opportunity to express myself in there in a way that allows me to reach a global audience in a world that duplicates my own. We even met once when I first joined up, because she used to hold technical lectures in Second Life as an avatar.

Second Life is a 3-D virtual world entirely built and owned by its residents, but the interpretation of that world changes depending on whom you ask. Some call it a game, some call it a creative medium (that describes me!), some call it the next evolution of the Internet, and for some, it's a place just as real as the world they live in. People create a likeness of themselves called an avatar; they meet others; buy and sell land, conduct business; and have relationships. It's a remarkable place where anything is possible and where real commerce with real money exchanges hands.

I took up residence and it happened to be Halloween. As soon as other avatars found out I was a real-life psychic medium, they wanted to hire me and pay me for readings. That payment was in "Lindens" (Second Life currency) but could be exchanged for real US dollars! With some borrowed clothes from someone else's inventory, I sat at a virtual table in this virtual world as people lined up for readings. Amazing to me was the fact that I could easily get lost in them, enough so as to bring through the other side *through the computer via avatars*! I was in a state of shock and immediately called to Watson (I mean Sue!) who came quickly to my Sherlock Holmes rescue. I told her that I needed someone to come "in-world" (the expression used when in Second Life) and help me line up the people for the readings and make sure they pay while I do the work.

Sue created her own account immediately. I often refer to her as "Sumi," so we used that for her first name and chose a last name from the list provided by Linden Lab, the software developer. She became Sumi Portola, got in-world, crashed several times (those were the early days of this new frontier and a lot of beta testing was going on), and then teleported her way to where I was in this vast community grid. Sumi got there via my Teleport Invitation, otherwise as a newbie she'd never be able to locate me in this exciting new world that had the huge potential to mirror our own.

It was not long before we set up several metaphysical centers and finally purchased an island for privacy sake, naming it Etu Abbracciare (Embrace You), in honor of my Italian heritage. We have created an extension of our Mountainside, New Jersey, Metaphysical Center in Second Life, and we refer to it as Embracing The Metaverse.

So now we had two global businesses and were expanding by providing products and services like: personal readings, guided meditations, and tools to work with spirit. We have become known as the leading, premier creators of Reiki healing tables and tools. Whatever you can get in real life, we can provide you with a virtual life version. This has been especially rewarding for me, personally, because I have been able to reach people regarding meditation and have fashioned items that work with animation in simulation.

Chapter Thirty-Eight

CRYSTAL VISIONS: MEETING MAX

······································

I FIRST LEARNED ABOUT Max, the Crystal Skull, as early as 1995 and had attended a group meditation with the ancient artifact in a New York City loft in 1997. I had always hoped that one day I would be able to host him for my clients, and that day was finally going to be upon us. I have hosted Max and his caretaker, JoAnn, three times: once from home as early as 2002 and then again in 2010 and 2011 at our metaphysical center.

During his visits, I have meditated alone with this historic artifact and shared meditation within a group. By opening my doors to a healing ancient vibration, I invited in a healing, uplifting energy for connecting body, mind, and spirit. You may have seen him on the posters for *Indiana Jones and the Kingdom of the Crystal Skull*, as he was used for some of the poster art with Harrison Ford in the movie. He is rare in that he is the only one authenticated crystal skull as a true artifact, and he travels the world to share with us.

Known nationally, Max is one of the thirteen original crystal skulls known in the world at this time.

As a "rock hound," I admit that this is my most exciting association with communicating with the energy we have available to us from the ages.

Authenticated by the British Museum, Max is at least ten thousand years old and weighs sixteen pounds. Max was found in a tomb in St. Augustine, Guatemala, in the 1920s and was used by Mayan priests for healing and prayer. What is even more astonishing is that he is not carved from any manmade tools, which lends further verification to him as an artifact.

The very idea of hosting him was electrifying because this crystal skull was in the possession of the Tibetan Red Hat Lama healer, Norbu Chen, when he went to Guatemala. He had visited with Mayan priests and was given the artifact. He traveled extensively, and one of those excursions took him to Houston, Texas. He began a healing foundation and positioned the crystal skull on the sacred space of his altar to use for healing and spiritual enlightenment. It is here that he met and befriended Max's present caretakers, JoAnn and Carl Parks, whose young daughter was in need of medical attention and healing at the time of their meeting. Though their daughter did not survive, JoAnn began working with the foundation. Before he passed away, Norbu Chen gifted the skull to JoAnn and Carl and offered no explanation. His only words were that when all was rightly aligned, the true nature of the crystal skull would be revealed. That message is one of peace, love, and unity.

I had the rare treat to be alone to have Max "sleep over" in my room on my end table by the bed. As is custom, I placed around him some of the jewelry I wanted "charged" with his energy and created a little sacred space right there beside me. I lit a candle and began to go into a meditation before bed. The room was literally buzzing with energy that was strong and clear and white. When I looked at Max on the table, his aura was white and lavender, and it was like a light show switching back and forth. My dreams were strong and vivid and included people who were using him as part of a shaman's healing ceremony. The atmosphere in the room was active and alive, which made it difficult to sleep through the night, but despite that I woke up refreshed and wrote the experience in my journal.

Todd, Jeffrey, and Sue had their private sessions, and our clients made appointments for the private and group sessions with Max, and it was a very enlightening event for all. It is rewarding for us to be able to open the doors of The Center for rare encounters like this. It restores an appreciation for those who have come before us, and the fact that we have people like JoAnn to travel and share with us was beyond special. As a way to contribute to our hosting of Max, the Crystal Skull, I made a video and incorporated photos of his last visit with the accompanying song, "Peace Train" by Cat Stevens because it expressed the message that I believe his chunk of healing quartz is all about. I have a fabulous picture I have included in this book that catches his aura on film that I took back in 2002.

Linda and Micky Dolenz

Linda Lauren (avatar)

Sumi Portola (avatar of Susan Dolinko)

Max, the Crystal Skull, Showing his Aura

Max, the Crystal Skull, with JoAnn Parks and The LLETU Team—Linda, Sue, Todd, and Jeffrey

Hostage in Time Book Signing

The Travel Psychic being interviewed in The LLETU Center

Linda and Her Dad (Pop)

Chapter Thirty-Nine

BEING HELD *HOSTAGE IN TIME*

······································

WRITING THE FICTIONAL time travel romance, *Hostage in Time,* was a labor of love for me, as I have always enjoyed reading a good time travel and wanted to write one myself. I can define 1979 to 1989 by the amount of time travel novels I had read. They were being released fast and furiously, and I was only too happy to lose myself in their pages. Aside from obvious choice of H. G. Wells, some of the great time travel romance authors include Constance O'Day-Flannery, Richard Matheson, and Jack Finney, all highly respected authors on the NY Times Bestsellers list. Some of you might recall the more mainstream work of Matheson, whose novel *Bid Time Return* was made into the popular film *Somewhere in Time*; Finney is known for his incredibly detailed work in *Time And Again*; and O'Day-Flannery has a string of some very wonderful novels, like *Second Chances.*

I have my own beliefs regarding the possibility of time travel. I have had two personal episodes and one astral travel experiment that add credence to my belief that traveling through time is possible. I had always fantasized about writing a story that incorporated the concept of time travel with my love of historic preservation and history.

From 1989 to 1999, I wrote and completed ten paranormal time travel romance novels, then placed each in its own manuscript box and put them in my office closet to await further action. *Hostage in Time* was the last one I finished. When my mother passed away that year and my practice got busier, another decade had gone by. It wasn't until 2011 that I found some time to update the manuscript for publication.

When I picked *Hostage in Time* up again, it was with wisdom I hadn't had when I first penned all that romance and mayhem! The fact that I now had the benefit of the technology of today to move my story forward allowed me to further enhance it to an exciting new level. I fell in love with the characters and the story all over again, wishing that I could be a guest at the fictional Serenity, enjoying the company of the Brisbane family.

The Merchant's House Museum

Once the book was published, we combed locations for the perfect place for the book launch. I wanted it to be the type of place that would represent time travel and life familiar to the period of 1884, while also appealing to myself as a psychic medium. We were elated to discover The Merchant's House Museum in Manhattan. The 1832 row house is one of the only homes built that has been perfectly preserved to the time period. It depicts home life in affluent, mid-nineteenth-century New York, where much of my novel takes place. Gertrude Tredwell was born in 1840 and lived in the house until she died in 1933, most of her days were spent in an upstairs bedroom. The moment I stepped across the threshold, it was as if I was being transported to her time.

We arranged for a private tour, and Eva, the curator, took us around, relating some of the ghost stories, real life stories of the family, and discussions regarding how we might utilize the facility. As Sue discussed those details, I continued my walk-through of the house. We were on the second floor, and I was standing in the middle of one of the bedrooms. Eva and Sue were not far behind me as I walked straight to a rocker, which sat next to, of all things, an oversized, white crib that was jammed next to a large dresser. Across from that was a bed designed for a very short person.

"This doesn't belong here," I said, pointing and frowning at the crib. I was standing in front of the rocker, and as I said the words, I could see the faint image of a woman begin to materialize, and she didn't look pleased. Let me interject here by saying that I am not jaded by the work I do. I am in awe that it even happens. I am amazed, grateful, shocked, and blessed every single time I get information or a spirit reveals him/herself to me, and I never take any of what I do for granted.

"That's correct. We moved it in here because of renovations. To be quite honest, we are not sure where a few of the items belong, so if you can help, that would be great."

I saw the woman shaking her head no, and she pointed to the door. I followed and walked across the hall to the other bedroom. "The dresser belongs here, in this room."

"Yes, that's where it was before we moved it."

"Well, then it was already in the right place." I turned and walked back to the bedroom with the crib. "The crib belongs to another house and may not be part of the Tredwell belongings. She doesn't want it here, and she wants the bedrooms to be correct in furniture placement." I looked at Eva and smiled. "She's very bossy!"

We started to walk together, Eva validating much of what I was saying about Ms. Tredwell, when, as we rounded the bed and headed toward the door to the stairs, we three came to a grinding halt.

"Do you see what I see?" I whispered.

"I see it." Sue had her camera out and was taking photos.

I stared, mesmerized by what appeared to be the rise and fall of the bedspread. "The bed looks like it's breathing."

The curator nodded and confirmed that she had seen it before, as had a paranormal investigator who had explored the house. We stood there for several long minutes as the outline of a body formed and then disappeared. I was chilled and could not wait to leave, but I knew we had found the place for the *Hostage in Time* book launch.

On the night of the event, we did our best to stick to the time period. There was a female servant dressed in

1884 garb answering the door, and the kitchen served food and wine of the era. It was a magical evening.

My father was alive at ninety to enjoy seeing it happen and even read the book, a page a day, while in the care center he was living in. I am grateful to have been able to make him smile and beam as he shared my book with the other residents.

Chapter Forty

TRAVEL PSYCHIC™

·····································

I HAVE ALWAYS HELPED people find the best routes, take the best means of transportation, close deals, sign documents, and deal with travel. It is a specialty that I didn't even realize was happening to me until an interview in 2011 by the *New York Times*. They labeled me the Travel Psychic™. I love saving people anxiety when traveling.

Interest in this aspect of my work draws a lot of attention because it gives people power over their agendas when they are away from home. I evaluate the color, energy, climate, feel, astrological considerations, and my client's personal energy in order to help them have the best trip possible. This garnished another visit from a studio to The Center. This one brought ABC and *Nightline* for a full day's interview for the show. Again, we were met with a crew who were respectful and left the place in the same condition as before they dismantled it for the interview. There was even a moment with one of the cameramen wherein his mother came through when I touched him, which made for a special day.

Those early days of helping one of my first clients with her trip to Italy was a catalyst and precursor, but another case comes to mind. This one involves a Wall Street power broker who traveled often overseas and sought my counsel on a regular basis to go over the dates of his itinerary.

On this particular visit, he told me he would be traveling to several places, among them, London and Dubai. I didn't see any red flags that would indicate worry except when it came to food. The journey itself would be a good one and would afford him new contacts and upgrade his business. However, his health was of major concern to me, and that surprised me because I do not consider myself to be a medical intuitive. I prefer to work in other areas, but I don't avoid giving a person a heads-up when I see one. In this case, I told him that I saw a picture in mind of him with a distended stomach.

"All I can say is be careful what you eat while away. I'm getting poor digestion that could warrant surgery if you're not careful."

He wrote this all down and thanked me.

A few months later, his wife gave us a call at The Center. She asked Sue to relay the message to me that her husband had eaten some bad food in Dubai. He had to be rushed into surgery, where work was done on his stomach. He sent me flowers and thanked me for the heads-up, but he was upset that he hadn't heeded the warning. That is when I explain to the client that we all have the power of choice, and just because I see something does not mean it is etched in stone.

It means it's "probable," and it is that probability that gives us the ability to explore the decisions. Whether those decisions are in our favor or not is entirely up to us.

Chapter Forty-One

THE VISIT—2012

....

I WAS SITTING WITH my father in the circular solarium of the care center he had been living in. He was in his nineties and in a talkative mood, full of stories to share that day. I take after him when it comes to verbalization. I was born talking, am still talking, and am now writing about what I talk about. He was the same way. Add to that the fact that he was overjoyed to be able to hear again after twenty years of personally denying himself a hearing aide, and you had all the earmarks of a "good" visit. I had a feeling that I was going to come away with some spectacular stories about our family. And I'm proud to say that I recorded his stories by microphone or video camera.

He looked up at me, his memory stirred, and he moved his wheelchair closer to where I sat. "You knew too much. You were too smart. We would hold a conversation with you like we would an adult." He laughed and then turned to my friend Sue. "She'd pin you down!"

"What would she do?" Sue asked.

He looked at me and shook his head. "She would pin people down to tell the truth about things because she knew more than they did!"

"Why do you think that was? Because I'm psychic like Grandma and Mom?"

"Maybe." He smiled here, deeply reminiscing. "You would go up to strangers and talk to them. My friend, Ernie, wouldn't talk to you because you made fun of him with the things that you knew. You told him things that he knew would get him in trouble. You would say things like, 'You have a girlfriend? What is she like?'"

My hand flew to my mouth. "But he was married, wasn't he...and to someone else?"

That set my father to laughing loud. "Oh, you embarrassed him!"

We were all laughing now as I slowly began to remember Ernie, but before I could muster up more than a vague image of him some fifty years ago, my father switched topics.

"I think you knew too much, and never stopped knowing too much. We always said she talks too much, but the funny thing is, even though she was just a baby, she knew what she was talking about, and that is what hurts. I would say, 'Linda, shut up,' and you would say, 'That's not nice to tell me to shut up. Don't tell me to shut up!' She was only about three or four years old. She came out talking!"

"And she's still talking," replied Sue, and I smiled as the two shared a belly laugh.

"She was in the crib, and she'd walk around...just walking around, talking to everyone in the room."

"But I was too young to talk—"

"Too young? No! You got it from somewhere!" He winked and laughed again. "You would come out with words we never heard, never mind any words we would ever hear come out of the mouth of a baby! You picked up on the energy of everyone who came to visit. You'd come out with a statement: 'That person said this or that...' and we would ask how you knew that, and you would shrug and say you just knew."

He was still talking, and I was beginning to tune him out. It was purely intentional; it's actually a survival technique I learned from Mom a while back. I could hear him telling my friend, Sue, about Winnie, The Walking Talking Doll he surprised me with for Christmas when I was five years old. The doll scared me when it came slowly sliding toward me on roller skates, singing with no mouth moving. If I was a teen, I could attribute it to being in an altered state, but, at five, I wasn't quite that rebel just yet. My mother called Winnie "Your Father's Sacrifice Gift." You must have had one of those in your life at one time or another. It's the gift your parent had to trek insurmountable miles knee deep in a freak snowstorm (the likes of which we had never seen) and against all odds, to buy a toy for his little tyke. Naturally, by the time he arrived, he was soaked through the bone, shivering and tired, only to be turned away by the owner of the store because they were closing! The story takes on additional chapters (and drama) each time it's told. I paid for every emotional moment that doll was in my life. Wait! I'm obviously still paying for it, because I'm mentioning it here, again.

"Winnie went to the doll hospital twice, and then she was put away in the closet," I could hear my father saying as I snapped back to present time, my mental rant a nostalgic memory of a long-ago past.

"And she stayed in my closet until I got married and left the house when I was twenty-one." I raised my hand to prevent Pop from finishing the story. "I don't want to know what you did with her—"

"Threw her out," he triumphantly announced. "Her, Debbie Reynolds, and Shirley Temple. In fact, the whole trunk…trashed."

A silence fell over the solarium room of visitors, and my father realized that he had said too much. "They had matted hair and were missing parts," he quickly explained.

But, it was really too late. Winnie, Debbie, and Shirley are in Dolly Heaven (unlike Dollywood). If they want to get a message to me, they know how to deliver it.

Chapter Forty-Two

NEW BEGINNINGS—
THANK YOU, POP

·······························

MY FATHER PASSED away on July 5, 2012, at the age of ninety-one. I was with him when his spirit left, and, after seeing him once or twice a week at the care center for those three years, I miss him even more. My father was a WWII veteran and had a military funeral. The morning after we buried him, a deer appeared in the backyard, trapped and looking for a way out. Deer denote love, beauty, wisdom, insight, and abundance. I thank God (and Pop) for the message.

And there have been others since he passed. Almost every day I receive a turtle sign. Turtles make me reflect back to my father's mother and that big turtle she used to have on a leash. It also relates to my other grandmother. So here we have turtles every day in some form. I usually take a screen shot and put it into my online journal along with what I feel the message of the day is. (That usually depends on the turtle image/saying.)

If you go to my website or my YouTube, you will find many of these stories of signs. There may be some helpful information for you to journalize and decipher your own signs by keeping track of them.

Afterword

A NOTE ON GRIEF

····································

ADDRESS THE COLORS of energy people are embracing, and I'm doing my best to help them redefine their personal palette. I believe the work I do is more that of an artist of the soul, as well as a psychic medium of the mind and spirit. We are all spirits with clean slates. There is always a fresh start from awareness and experience. But all awareness is not negative, nor experience necessarily bad. When we suffer a personal loss, we propel our energy into defense mode, guard up and tears down. It is the one time we truly feel permitted to experience open emotion, and that can either make us stronger or weaker, depending upon our approach.

We all have to go through the emotion of grief on this planet at this time because that is what is expected of us in this society. Depending upon your background or belief system, death is considered a celebration of life or a mourning of passing. There are no rules, except perhaps the traditions of our family, which bind us to experience mourning a loved one in one complete way. This boggles my mind! How can one's experience truly equal that of another? We are all the same, yet different, and our DNA pattern is not just scientific but relative to a higher nature: one of the soul.

Because we are all energy and information, we each hold a different vibration that connects us to another. How can one person's experience with death even come close to that of another's? It has to be gauged and put into perspective; and even if there is no real way to gauge it, we have available to us the ways and means of working through grief and moving forward. Then what we have defined as "obstacles" (like memories and places shared with the loved one) become stepping-stones with positive references and results that help create a healthy experience out of the loss.

PS to My Readers:

I thank you for reading what I've had to say, and I feel blessed to be able to share what I have experienced and learned about the work I do. Admittedly, this book took a lot out of me personally, because I came to continue the writing process after my father died. It is part of my healing, and I have all of you to embrace and be grateful to for that. Remember to keep the right thought and love in your heart, and the sun will always shine for you.

God bless and love,

Linda